Monitor Lizards A

Monitor Lizard Comprehensi

Monitor Lizard care, behavior, enclosures, feeding, health, myths and interaction all included.

by

Marvin Murkett and Ben Team

ALL RIGHTS RESERVED. This book contains material protected under International and Federal Copyright Laws and Treaties.

Any unauthorized reprint or use of this material is strictly prohibited. No part of this book may be reproduced or transmitted in any form or by any means, electronic, mechanical or otherwise, including photocopying or recording, or by any information storage and retrieval system without express written permission from the author.

Copyrighted © 2015

Published by: IMB Publishing

Table of Contents

About The Authors 8

Foreword 9

Chapter 1: Monitor Lizard Description and Anatomy 14

    Size 14

    Color, Pattern and Scalation 14

    Skeletal System 15

    Internal Organs 15

    Reproductive Organs 15

    Head 16

    Eyes 16

    Ears 16

    Tongue, Nose and Vomeronasal Organ 17

    Mouth and Teeth 18

    Venom and Toxic Saliva 19

    Vent 19

    Tail 20

Chapter 2: Monitor Lizard Biology and Behavior 21

    Biology 21

Chapter 3: Classification and Taxonomy 28

Chapter 4: The Monitor Lizard's World 32

    Range 32

    Habitat 32

    Natural Diet 33

    Natural Predators 33

Chapter 5: Monitor Lizards as Pets 35

Understanding the Commitment 35

The Costs of Captivity 35

Myths and Misunderstandings 40

Acquiring Your Monitor Lizard 41

Selecting Your Monitor Lizard 43

Quarantine 47

Chapter 6: Providing the Captive Habitat **48**

Enclosure 48

Chapter 7: Establishing the Thermal Environment **53**

Thermal Gradients 53

Heat Lamps 54

Ceramic Heat Emitters 55

Radiant Heat Panels 56

Heat Pads 57

Heat Tape 57

Heat Cables 58

Hot Rocks 58

Thermometers 59

Thermostats and Rheostats 60

Nighttime Heating 63

Incorporating Thermal Mass 63

Chapter 8: Lighting the Enclosure **65**

Chapter 9: Substrate and Furniture **69**

Substrate 69

Substrates to Avoid 71

Cage Furniture 72

Chapter 10: Maintaining the Captive Habitat **78**

Cleaning Procedures 78

Chemicals & Tools 79

Keeping Records 81

Common Husbandry Problems and Solutions 85

Chapter 11: Feeding Monitor Lizards 87

Insects 87

Fish 87

Rodents 87

Birds 88

Eggs 88

Live, Fresh Killed or Frozen 88

Prey Size 89

How to Offer Food 89

Feeding Frequency 90

Safety at Feeding Time 92

Chapter 12: Hydrating Your Monitor Lizard 93

Drinking Water 93

Humidity 93

Soaking Your Lizard 95

Chapter 13: Interacting with Monitor Lizards 96

Handling 96

In The Event of a Bite 96

Temporary Transport Cages 97

Transporting Tips 97

Hygiene 97

Chapter 14: Common Health Concerns 98

Finding a Suitable Veterinarian 98

Reasons to Visit the Veterinarian 99

Common Health Problems *99*

Chapter 15: Breeding Monitor Lizards 107

Sexing Monitor Lizards *107*

Pre-Breeding Conditioning *108*

Cycling *109*

Pairing *110*

Gravid *110*

Egg Deposition *111*

Egg Incubation *111*

Neonatal Husbandry *112*

Chapter 16: Good Pet Species 113

Suitable Pet Species of the Odatria Complex *113*

Suitable Pet Species of the Euprepiosaurus Subgenus *114*

Suitable Pet Species of the Polydaedalus Subgenus *116*

Suitable Pet Species of the Varanus Subgenus *116*

Chapter 17: Generally Inappropriate Pet Species 118

Nile Monitors *118*

Water Monitors *119*

Crocodile Monitors *119*

"New" Euprepiosaurus Species *119*

Chapter 18: Further Reading 121

Books *121*

Magazines *123*

Websites *123*

Journals *125*

Supplies *125*

Support Organizations *126*

References...**127**

About The Authors

Marvin Murkett is an experienced writer and a true animal lover. He has been keeping reptiles and amphibians for over 30 years. He enjoys writing animal books and advising others how to take care of their animals to give them a happy home.

Ben Team is an environmental educator and author with over 16 years of professional reptile-keeping experience.

Ben currently maintains www.FootstepsInTheForest.com, where he shares information, narration and observations of the flora, fauna and habitats of Metro Atlanta.

While he thoroughly enjoys writing about the natural world, Ben's favorite moments are those spent in the company of his beautiful wife.

Foreword

Unlike snakes, who also swallow impressively large prey, *they* are active predators, who spend considerable time exploring their cages, looking for hidden edibles.

Unlike many iguanas, who also reach large sizes, *they* exude intelligence. They dig, manipulate, explore and explode into movement when necessary, rather than lazily plucking leaves and fruit from their dish before returning to their perch to sleep.

Unlike so many skinks, collared lizards and whiptails, who are also skilled and impressive predators of local ecosystems, *they* include the largest lizards in the world among their ranks.

They, of course, are monitor lizards. Arguably, the most desirable, fascinating and fulfilling pets in the world.

***

Although they are not closely related to the dinosaurs, monitor lizards evoke the same feelings of awe and wonder that they do. Although most modern monitor species are less than a million years old or so, many other species have been documented from fossil beds more than 70 million years old.

One relatively recent, but currently extinct, species grew over 20 feet long. These giant lizards – known to herpetologists as Varanus priscus -- lived in Australia as recently as 250,000 years ago.

Early human settlers of Australia must have feared these giant beasts, who would certainly have preyed upon any humans they encountered. Fortunately for those currently living in Australia, the giant lizards became extinct relatively shortly after humans arrived in Australia.

Whether humans played a role in the species' extinction or not is not yet clear.

***

Scientists recognize over 70 different species in the genus Varanus. Five of these species derive significant protection and essentially absent from the pet trade. Another 30 or so species are not represented in the pet trade. Of the remaining species, perhaps half are at all appropriate for amateur reptile enthusiasts.

Among other traits of those species that are well suited for captivity, most that make good pets are rather small. New hobbyists should seek out species that remain less than 3 feet long, such as many of the "dwarf" monitors.

Even keepers with some experience should stick to species of 4 or 5 feet. The largest specimens of the largest species grow massive enough that they represent a significant safety threat, and are only suitable for the most experienced keepers, with adequate resources to provide a high quality of life for such incredible – but potentially hazardous – animals.

Even the smallest monitor lizards need roomy cages to permit enough room for exercise, the establishment of thermal and photo gradients and a high quality of life. For small species, this means constructing or purchasing a large cage; for large species this means dedicating a medium-sized room to your pet – complete with walls, floors and windows fortified to be "monitor-proof."

The largest monitor lizards can undoubtedly maim or kill humans. Although it is rare, large Komodo dragons occasionally predate upon people, and several species have been observed feeding on human corpses. A 6-foot-long Nile or Water monitor can inflict serious wounds, and deserve as much respect as would be afforded a crocodilian of similar length. Crocodile monitors, who are the longest, if not largest, species in the genus, have exceptionally horrifying dentition and have occasionally inflicted serious injuries on their keepers.

Clearly, caution is warranted whenever considering pets with this type of capability.

In stark contrast to the large species, many of the dwarf monitors are *relatively* harmless. They may still scratch the hand that holds them, or bite the fingers that feed them, but these bites are often relatively mild – on par with a nip from a small dog, turtle or hamster. Care should certainly be employed, and they should not be handled by children or allowed to be close to the handler's face.

***

Many monitor lizard species are experiencing sharp population declines in the wild. This is occurring for a number of reasons, including habitat destruction, exploitation for the leather trade and over collection for the pet trade.

While the number of monitors killed by the first two factors undoubtedly dwarf the number that are removed from the wild for the pet trade, hobbyists – who presumably appreciate the role these lizards play in the wild – should be keen to act in the best interests of monitor lizards.

This means that, whenever possible, hobbyists should seek out and acquire captive bred lizards, which place no strain on wild populations. Additionally, captive bred monitors are far more likely to thrive in captivity than wild caught monitors are.

This is not only due to the stress that wild caught animals suffer from while being transported across the world, bouncing from one facility to the next. Wild caught monitor lizards are invariably loaded with parasites; their stressful trip to North American or European shores only exacerbates this problem.

Unfortunately, some species are not bred regularly in captivity. Accordingly, those who wish to work with some of these species are limited to dealing with wild-caught animals.

When this is necessary, be sure to purchase only those animals that are legal to own in your area (many jurisdictions restrict the ownership of large monitors) and were legally obtained.

***

While herpetologists have learned a great deal about monitor lizards in the past few decades, much remains to be learned.

As recently as 1998, Daniel Bennett's important work *Monitor Lizards: Natural History, Biology and Husbandry*, listed 45 described species. Today, that number has climbed to 74. While some of these species were already known to science, and have simply been reclassified, many have been documented for the first time in the last 20 years.

These are not all small, obscure and easily overlooked species. Many of them -- such as the bitatawa monitors (*Varanus bitatawa*) of the Philippines, who were first documented in 2010 -- reach 5 feet in length.

In a world where species are disappearing at an alarming rate, such discoveries are both surprising and exciting. With any luck, even more species will be discovered in the future.

This highlights the importance of protecting the world's habitats. Who knows how many other species await discovery.

***

Monitors go by a variety of names that vary from one place to the next. While scientists often call them Varanids, or use their scientific names to identify specific species, laypersons often call them monitor lizards. In Australia, the term "goanna" replaces the term "monitor lizard."

In all cases, those people who live alongside these large lizards have introduced the lizards to their culture, mythologies and creation myths.

Many members of developing countries hold false beliefs about the lizards. For example, desert monitors are often considered venomous by tribal peoples of North Africa, although herpetologists know that this is not the case.

Chapter 1: Monitor Lizard Description and Anatomy

Although they vary in a number of relatively subtle ways, monitor lizards all have a similar basic body plan. They are elongate, four-limbed lizards with long necks and long, powerful tails. Some species have body plans at the lithe end of the spectrum, while others are stouter in build.

Size

Monitor lizards vary greatly in size. Short-tailed monitors (*Varanus brevicauda*) are the smallest species, and they rarely exceed 1/20 of a pound (20 grams) in weight. By contrast, Komodo dragons (*Varanus komodoensis*) may weigh up to 150 pounds (69 kilograms) or more.

In general, monitor lizards fall into one of three general size classes:

- Small species, which are less than 3 feet in total length
- Medium-sized species, which are between 3 and 5 feet in length
- Large species, which grow longer than 5 feet

Color, Pattern and Scalation

Monitor lizards exhibit a wide range of colors and patterns, but most are earth-toned animals with contrasting spots or bands. Nevertheless, green, blue, yellow, orange and red tones appear on some species.

Most monitor lizards have very high-contrast patterns when they are young, but these become more muted over time. For example, hatchling water monitors are quite gaudy, clad in black and gold bands. However, many adult water monitors only display the faintest hints of banding.

Brown rough-necked monitors exhibit one of the greatest examples of color change – the young have bright orange heads for about the first six weeks of their lives. To date, no satisfactory hypothesis has been proposed to explain this phenomenon.

Skeletal System

Varanid skeletons largely resemble those of humans and other vertebrates. As with most other reptiles, birds and mammals, they have an axial skeleton, composed of the skull, ribs and vertebrae, and an appendicular skeleton, composed of the shoulder and pelvic girdles, as well as the bones of the limbs and feet.

Their vertebral column extends through their tails, which bear no fracture planes, as is common in some other lizard species. This means that they do not drop their tails, nor do they regenerate if lost.

Varanids and their close relatives, Bornean earless lizards, are unique among lizards in having nine cervical vertebrae; all other lizards have necks comprised of eight or fewer vertebrae. (Ast, n.d.)

Monitors have rather robust skulls that allow for the attachment of large jaw and neck muscles.

Internal Organs

Monitor lizard anatomy differs relatively little from that of other lizards, or tetrapods in general. Their digestive system is comprised of an esophagus, stomach, small intestine, large intestine and a terminal chamber called the cloaca. They also have gall bladders and livers that serve similar purposes as they do in other vertebrates.

Monitor lizards control their bodies via their brain and nervous system. Their endocrine and exocrine glands work much as they do in other vertebrates.

Kidneys filter wastes in the monitor's bloodstream, while their heart pumps blood that their lungs oxygenate.

Reproductive Organs

Like all squamates, male monitor lizards have paired reproductive organs, called hemipenes. When not in use, males keep their hemipenes inside the base of their tails. When they attempt to mate with a female, they evert one of the hemipenes and insert it into the female's cloaca.

The paired nature of the male sex organs ensure that males can continue to breed if they suffer injury to one of the hemipenes.

Females have paired ovaries and oviducts, which store the eggs after they are released from the ovaries. The eggs are shelled and held inside the oviducts until it is time to deposit the eggs. At this time, the eggs are passed from the oviducts into the cloaca and out of the body via the vent.

Head

In general, monitor lizards have massive, strong heads. However, the head of each species has evolved to suit its lifestyle. Those that eat large prey tend to have larger, more robust heads, while insect-eating species often have elongate, delicate heads.

Eyes

Monitor lizards have very good eyesight. While their chemically oriented senses (taste, smell, vomeronasal) are perhaps more important to the animals' survival, monitors use their vision to help detect predators, prey and mates, among other resources.

It is not clear if monitors are able to distinguish colors or not, but they are able to spot movement at very long distances. Anecdotal data suggests that some monitors can detect predators at up to 200 meters away.

The eyes of monitors are fixed in their eye sockets and unable to rotate. They possess a horizontal eyelid – nictitating membrane – although it is rarely seen in captive lizards, given the speed with which it moves.

Monitors cannot see in complete darkness, although they see adequately in dim light.

Ears

Monitor lizards have rather unremarkable ears. They are composed chiefly of an opening in the lizard's skull across which the tympanic membrane stretches. Internally, their ears are structured much as the ears of other lizards are.

Hearing is likely the least acute sense of monitor lizards. They can hear, but often fail to react to relatively loud noises. Field biologists have noted that it is not as necessary to be quiet when attempting to remain stealthy around monitors, as it is to remain out of their line of sight and downwind of them.

Tongue, Nose and Vomeronasal Organ

The tongue, nose and vomeronasal organ all work in conjunction to detect chemical clues from the lizard's environment. Monitor lizards repeatedly flick their bifurcated tongues, much as snakes do. The tongue tips collect volatile substances and transport them back into the mouth.

Once the tongue tips are in the mouth, they place the collected chemicals in two small holes in the roof of the mouth. These holes are the exterior opening to a structure called the Jacobson's organ. The Jacobson's organ transmits the clues contained in the chemicals collected by the tongue to the brain, where they are interpreted.

The dorsal surface of the tongue of monitor lizards is rough, but it serves no role in feeding. (Smith, 2005)

The nostrils of monitors function largely as the nostrils of other lizards do. However, the placement and shape of the nostrils of each species varies.

For example, many aquatic or semi-aquatic species, such as Merten's water monitors, mangrove monitors and brown rough-necked monitors, have valve-like nostrils. These lizards can seal their nostrils to prevent water from entering them during extended dives.

The nostrils of many aquatic species, such as Nile monitors, are placed in a location that allows the lizards to breathe while much of their head remains underwater.

Other monitors have nostrils that are located nearer the eyes, which helps them to smell prey below ground when they are pressing their heads into the substrate. This is characteristic of several species, but savannah monitors are perhaps the best example.

The forked tongues of monitor lizards are often surprisingly long.

Mouth and Teeth

Monitor lizards have a large number of sharp teeth, although they often remain hidden by the gum tissue. When they bite down on something, their teeth emerge from the gums and penetrate the flesh or shell of their prey.

Monitors shed and replace their teeth throughout their lives. You may occasionally find shed teeth in your animal's droppings. Some keepers have reported instances in which geriatric monitors failed to replace their teeth as quick as they had earlier in life.

Different species of monitor lizard have different types of teeth. Those species that feed heavily on insects tend to have sharp, pointed teeth. Those that feed on mollusks and other shelled prey often have broad, flat molars that help them to crush their prey.

Komodo dragons have shark-like, serrated teeth that have evolved to rip and tear flesh. Crocodile monitors are equipped with long, conical teeth that resemble fangs. Although it is not clear what the purpose of these long teeth is, many scientists hypothesize that they are an adaptation that allows the tree-dwelling monitors to consume birds.

Interestingly, many monitors exhibit ontogenetic (age related) shifts in their dentition. For example, many of the African monitors – notably Nile and savannah monitors – have sharp teeth as juveniles. This is appropriate for the young lizards, who primarily consume insects and very small vertebrates.

However, as the lizards mature, they develop broad molars that are capable of crushing snails, which are ubiquitous in their natural habitats. (Williams, 1984)

Venom and Toxic Saliva
Herpetologists have long known that bites from Komodo dragons often become very infected. In many cases, animals that receive a bite from a Komodo dragon die, even if they escape.

The monitor lizards use this to their advantage, as they will bite a large prey animal and wait for them to die. Shortly afterwards, the monitors seek out the carcass and begin feeding.

Until recently, the lizards were not thought to be venomous – instead, they were thought to harbor a virulent cocktail of bacteria in their mouths, which caused the death in their prey. However, herpetologists working with the lizards have found that Komodo dragons do indeed possess venom. (Brian G. Fry, 2008)

While no other monitors are thought to possess venom at this time, it is possible that venom will be isolated from other species in the future. Lace monitors are of considerable interest to many researchers, as they have serrated teeth, which resemble those of Komodo dragons in many respects.

Vent
Monitor lizards have a small opening – called the vent – on their ventral surface, near the base of the tail. The vent leads directly to the cloaca, and serves as the final exit point for waste, urates and eggs.

When lizards defecate, release urates or copulate, the vent opens slightly. Some males evert their hemipenes during defecation.

Tail

Monitor lizards have long, muscular tails that serve a variety of purposes. Most exhibit adaptations suitable for the species' habitat or lifestyle.

For example, many aquatic species – notably mangrove, water and Nile monitors – have dorsolaterally flattened tails that help to propel them through the water. Arboreal species often have strongly prehensile tails, while those of spiny-tailed monitors bear sharp spines that serve defensive functions.

All monitors undoubtedly benefit from the balance afforded by their tail, but it may make them faster as well. Many lizards that drop their tails are faster with intact tails than they are without them.

Monitor lizards do not have tails that regenerate, but wild specimens frequently sustain damage to their tails over time. Some may be missing part of their tail, but it generally poses no serious threat to the lizard's health.

Chapter 2: Monitor Lizard Biology and Behavior

Now that you have some idea of the components that form monitor lizards, it is important to understand how those components work together and how the lizards behave.

Biology

The living monitors exhibit a range of lifestyles, diets and habitats, but their biology is relatively similar throughout the group.

For keepers of these interesting reptiles, some of the most important aspects of their biology include:

- Monitor lizards are ectothermic, meaning that their body temperature is dependent upon external sources of heat.
- All but a few species are obligate carnivores; most species are highly opportunistic, and they will take virtually any prey they can catch.
- Monitor lizards are long-lived by lizard standards, and some species reach 20 years of age or more.
- Monitor lizards are usually very swift, strong and athletic lizards that can maintain activity levels for extended time periods.
- Monitor lizards in many locations become dormant for six months of the year or longer, when environmental conditions are not favorable. Others, who live in tropical locations, remain active all year long.

Shedding

Like virtually all other animals, monitor lizards must discard and replace old skin cells. However, unlike snakes, who usually shed their skin in one piece, monitor lizards often shed in numerous patches. This often causes monitor lizards to retain portions of shed skin for lengthy periods of time.

In fact, it is not uncommon to see monitor lizards with multiple layers of shed skin on their bodies. However, this is not desirable, and proper husbandry should eliminate this problem. Usually, retained skin persists on the back, where it causes the lizard relatively little trouble. However, if they retain skin around the tail tip, eyes or toes, they can develop health problems.

Metabolism and Digestion
Monitors have relatively quick digestive rates when provided with appropriate temperatures. While monitor lizards do not require mammal-like quantities of food, they do require more frequent feedings than snakes or crocodiles.

Growth Rate and Lifespan
Monitor lizards are capable of relatively rapid growth. Most small species become mature in their second or third season, while large species may take 8 years of more before reaching sexual maturity.

Monitors exhibit varying lifespans – in general, the larger species live longer than smaller species do. Most probably reach 10 years of age or more. Some of the maximum-recorded ages for captive monitors are listed below.

- Komodo Dragon – 25 years
- Perentie Monitor – 19 years
- Brown Rough-Necked Monitor – 10 years
- Timor Monitor – 14 years

Monitor lizards undoubtedly live longer in captivity (when provided with appropriate care) than they do in the wild.

Behavior
While there is some variation between the different species, most monitor lizards spend their nights sleeping in a secure place, such as a burrow, rock crevice or tree hollow. In the morning, monitors emerge from their overnight retreats.

Some species begin foraging immediately, while others must first bask in the sun to raise their body temperature high enough to permit activity.

After foraging, monitor lizards usually retreat to their shelter (usually a different retreat than the one used previously). They may re-emerge after the heat of the mid-day sun has passed, or simply remain in their burrow for the remainder of the day.

In addition to foraging, male monitor lizards may spend extended periods of time seeking out mates.

Foraging

Monitor lizards obtain food in a wide variety of ways. Most are entirely carnivorous, but fruit comprises the bulk of the diet of Bitatawa, Panay and Gray's monitors. They prefer oily fruits, and they often inhabit trees that produce these favored fruits. A few keepers have found that green tree monitors and a few other species will consume fruit, but it is not known if this is an artifact of captivity or representative of natural behavior.

Generally speaking, small monitor lizards prey on invertebrates and elongate ectothermic prey, while larger species include rodents, birds and carrion in their diet.

A few species exhibit somewhat specialized feeding adaptations, such as brown rough-necked monitors, who appear to have shell-piercing teeth and other adaptations that enable them to collect crabs from mangrove forests.

Most monitor lizards forage by searching widely while using their senses – primarily vision, smell and taste – until they locate suitable prey. Once spotted, monitor lizards grasp prey with their mouths and either consume it immediately or thrash it and press the animal into the substrate until it stops fighting back or trying to flee. The food is then swallowed whole.

Scientists have not yet determined the manner in which monitor lizards search for food. Some appear to have no defined strategy, seemingly searching wherever their journeys take them; whereas others search out archetypal locations, such as dung, termite mounds or rodent burrows.

Unlike most other monitors, large Komodo dragons may ambush prey by hiding along game trails. Sometimes these giant lizards kill prey that weighs as much as 15 times their body weight.

Typically, monitor lizards forage in the same habitats in which they spend most of their time. For example, arboreal species, such as green tree monitors, Gray's monitors and crocodile monitors, catch their prey in trees. Similarly, rock-dwelling species, such as Kimberly rock goannas, capture their prey amid the same rock piles they inhabit.

Nevertheless, monitor lizards are very flexible animals, and some develop unique foraging strategies. Some populations of water monitors undertake daily journeys from forest canopies, where they avoid predators during the night, to aquatic habitats, where they catch prey.

All monitors have excellent chemically oriented senses, and they often find hidden food. Some species, notably savannah monitors and yellow monitors, have nostrils located in places that prevent dirt from entering and clogging them.

Diel Activity
Most monitor lizards are exclusively diurnal. Nevertheless, a few scattered observations exist detailing monitor lizards moving at night. The black-palmed goanna is one exception, as they are routinely observed foraging after dark. This has led some to label them as "twilight goannas." Additionally, water monitors and Komodo dragons have been observed foraging under moonlit skies from time to time.

They tend to become active early in the morning in areas with suitably warm temperatures, or as soon as basking allows them to attain suitable temperatures for activity.

Seasonal Activity
While some monitors live in equatorial forests, and experience relatively little seasonal changes, those living in Southern Africa, parts of Asia and Australia may have to cope with changing seasons.

In general, monitors respond to extremely hot (or dry) conditions in the same way that they respond to cold conditions – they take shelter in a burrow, tree hollow or similar place until more comfortable temperatures return.

Yellow monitors, for example, inhabit very seasonal habitats in South Asia. During the rainy summertime, the animals are active, forage frequently, mate and deposit eggs. However, during the cold, dry winters, these lizards retreat to deep rock crevices and other forms of shelter for several months.

Desert monitors are also subjected to incredible seasonal variation, although the specific environmental fluctuations vary across this species' vast range. Most seek shelter and become dormant when temperatures and rainfall levels are not appropriate. Some desert monitors even utilize two different active seasons – a relatively long active period during the spring and early summer, followed by a short period of inactivity and then a brief activity period in the fall.

Additionally, Bengal monitors, Rosenberg's goannas, white-throated monitors, Nile monitors and Lace goannas all inhabit areas that are at the latitudinal extremes for the genus, and may experience well-defined seasonal changes.

Many monitors that live in highly seasonal climates must fast for several months while temperatures are too low for digestion. (Phillips, 1997)

Defensive Strategies and Tactics
Most monitor lizards have a variety of predators, although large Komodo dragons and other gigantic monitors fear few predators but humans. Perhaps not unexpectedly, they have evolved a number of defense mechanisms to reduce the threat of predation.

The first line of defense employed by essentially all monitors is avoiding detection. They accomplish this behaviorally by staying in sheltered locations as much as possible and limiting the amount of time they spend exposed; but almost all monitors have evolved color patterns that provide effective camouflage.

Once discovered, most monitor lizards will attempt to flee. Given their impressive speed, the technique is often effective, as anyone who has tried to catch a monitor lizard in open territory already knows. They usually attempt to reach some type of shelter, but they may climb to safety or enter the water and swim away.

In fact, monitors can stay underwater for lengthy periods of time while waiting for predators to leave. Nile monitors, for example, are able to remain underwater for more than 1 hour. (Stephen C. Wood, 1974)

If cornered and unable to reach a safe retreat, monitor lizards often unleash a barrage of intimidation techniques. They will stand as tall as possible and position their body perpendicularly to the threat. They may hiss, gape their mouths or breathe heavily (and audibly).

If the threat is not dissuaded by these displays, most monitor lizards – particularly larger species – will attempt to slap the antagonist with their tails. Some species appear to their tail tips toward their attacker's face and eyes.

If the attacker grasps the lizard, it is likely to be met with a powerful bite. The lizards may also use their claws to scratch the threat as well. Monitor lizards may also defecate or release urates and water to deter predators. Interestingly, it is not only the large monitor species that engage in bluffing behaviors, such as hissing and lunging. Even the smallest species – which cannot harm a human-sized predator significantly – engage in these behaviors.

Locomotion
Monitor lizards are very athletic animals that can traverse a wide array of substrates with little trouble. All species can theoretically climb, but large Komodo dragons rarely do and the short-toed, yellow monitor is not a skilled climber.

When walking, monitors flex their bodies from one side to the other, which extends their reach. In other words, when a monitor reaches forward with its front left limb, it bends its body so that its left shoulder is moved forward.

Monitor lizards can reach high speeds when sufficiently warm. Most species easily outpace humans over short distances, but given the limits of their cold-blooded metabolism, they will tire much more quickly than a healthy human will. (TODD T. GLEESON)

Many of the tree monitors – especially the green tree monitors and their close relatives -- use their dexterous tails to grip branches. However, even large-bodied species, such as lace, water and white-throated monitors can scurry up a tree with amazing quickness.

Many juvenile monitors spend the majority of their time in the trees, presumably to avoid terrestrial predators.

Reproduction
Relatively little is known about wild monitor lizard breeding habits. The males of most species appear to engage in wide-ranging mate-seeking behaviors, while females tend to have smaller home ranges. However, these generalizations may be biased in that only a few species have been studied in detail.

Males are usually larger than females are, and they often engage in combat to establish dominance.

Monitor lizards mate similarly to most other lizards, with the male approaching the female from behind, and bending her tail upward to allow cloacal juxtaposition and ultimately, intercourse and fertilization.

Females deposit their eggs several weeks later in a thermally stable place. Many species bury their eggs in the substrate, but some deposit their eggs inside termite mounds, where the actions of the tiny insects and the design of their mound keep the eggs relatively safe and warm.

When the young hatch from their eggs, they are on their own – no maternal care is given subsequent to egg deposition.

Chapter 3: Classification and Taxonomy

The taxonomy of monitor lizards has changed numerous times, and will likely to continue to change for the foreseeable future. While all monitor lizards are clearly closely related, the finer points of their classification remain controversial. Additionally, the interrelationships between monitor lizards and their closest relatives are not completely clear.

In the last twenty years, the number of described monitor species has nearly doubled. A 1994 study published in the "Australian Journal of Ecology," by monitor lizard legend Eric Pianka, noted 40 described species. Currently, taxonomists recognize 74 living monitor species and dozens of subspecies.

As currently construed, all 74 described monitor lizard species are grouped in the genus *Varanus*, which is the only genus within the family Varanidae.

The family Varanidae combines with the family Lanthanotidae, which contains a single species – the Bornean earless lizard (*Lanthanotus borneensis*) – and the family Helodermatidae, which includes Gila monsters (*Heloderma suspectum*) and Mexican beaded lizards (*Heloderma horridum*), to form the infraorder Platynota. Some authorities use the name Varanoidea, instead.

Perentie goannas are the largest Australian monitors.

Some authorities recognize several different sub-genera within the genus *Varanus*.

Polydaedalus	*albigularis*	White-Throated Monitor
	niloticus	Nile Monitor
	exanthematicus	Savannah Monitor
	yemenensis	Yemen Monitor
	ornatus	Ornate Monitor
Psammosaurus	*griseus*	Desert Monitor
Empagusia	bengalensis	Bengal Monitor
	flavescens	Yellow Monitor
	dumerilii	Brown Roughneck Monitor
	rudicollis	Black Roughneck Monitor
	nebulosus	Clouded Monitor
Varanus	*komodoensis*	Komodo Dragon
	varius	Lace Goanna
	giganteus	Perentie Goanna
	mertensi	Mertens' Water Goanna
	rosenbergi	Heath Goanna
	flavirufus	Desert Sand Goanna
	gouldii	Sand Goanna
	panoptes	Yellow-Spotted Goanna
	spenceri	Spencer's Goanna
Soterosaurus	*salvator*	Water Monitor
	marmoratus	Luzon Water Monitor
	cumingi	Cuming's Water Monitor
	nuchalis	Rough-Necked Water Monitor
	rasmusseni	Rasmussen's Water Monitor
	togianus	Black Water Monitor
	palawanensis	Palawan Island Water Monitor

Papusaurus	*salvadorii*	Crocodile Monitor
Odatria	*mitchelli*	Mitchell's Goanna
	auffenbergi	Auffenberg's Goanna
	baritji	Black-Spotted Ridge-Tailed Goanna
	bushi	Bush's Dwarf Goanna
	caudolineatus	Line-Tailed Goanna
	gilleni	Pygmy Mulga Goanna
	primordius	Northern Blunt-Spined Goanna
	hamersleyensis	Southern Pilbara Rock Goanna
	timorensis	Timor Monitor
	scalaris	Banded Tree Monitor
	acanthurus	Ridge-Tailed Goanna
	brevicauda	Short-Tailed Goanna
	glauerti	Kimberly Rock Goanna
	glebopalma	Black-Palmed Rock Goanna
	pilbarensis	Pilbara Goanna
	eremius	Rusty Desert Goanna
	similis	*Spotted Tree Monitor*
	semiremex	Rusty Goanna
	storri	Storr's Goanna
	tristis	Black-Tailed Goanna
	kingorum	Pygmy Rock Goanna
Philippinosaurus	*bitatawa*	Bitatawa Monitor
	mabitang	Panay Monitor
	olivaceus	Gray's Monitor

Euprepiosaurus	*indicus*	Mangrove Monitor
	jobiensis	Peach-Throated Monitor
	doreans	Blue-Tailed Monitor
	prasinus	Green Tree Monitor
	beccarii	Black Tree Monitor
	boehmei	Bohme's Black Tree Monitor
	Bogerti	Bogert's Monitor
	cerambonensis	Ceram Monitor
	caerulivirens	Turquiose Monitor
	finschi	Finsch's Monitor
	juxtindicus	Rennell Island Monitor
	kordensis	Biak Island Tree Monitor
	lirungensis	Talaud Mangrove Monitor
	keithhornei	Nesbit River Goanna
	macraei	Blue-Spotted Tree Monitor
	melinus	Quince Monitor
	obor	Torch-Faced Monitor
	rainerguentheri	Gunther's Monitor
	reisingeri	Reisinger's Monitor
	telenesetes	Mysterious Tree Monitor
	yuwonoi	Tri-Colored Monitor
	zugorum	Zug's Monitor
	spinulosus	Solomon Island Spiny Monitor

Chapter 4: The Monitor Lizard's World

To maintain a monitor lizard successfully, you must understand his native habitat and functionally replicate it.

Range

Monitor lizards are restricted to the Old World, where they inhabit most of Africa, Southern Asia and Australia.

Millions of years ago, monitor lizards inhabited a much greater portion of the world. Paleontologists have found fossils from monitor lizards in the United States, Canada and North Asia.

Monitor lizards do not occur in Madagascar or Tasmania. Humans have introduced a few species outside their natural range. Currently, feral monitor populations occur in Guam and the Florida Everglades.

Habitat

Monitor lizards live in a wide variety of habitats. Several species inhabit the deserts of North Africa, Southwest Asia and the arid Australian Interior; while the rainforests of Southeast Asia and Northern Australia are also home to many monitor species.

Some live in the mangrove swamps of Southeast Asia and Australia, while others prefer the savannahs of Africa. Many inhabit islands that have no larger predators, and some have learned to thrive in urban areas.

Some wide-ranging species inhabit several different habitats, while some species are restricted to a single island, covered in relatively homogeneous habitat.

In all cases, the monitors must be able to acquire their basic needs, including food, shelter and water, from their habitat. Additionally, because they are ectothermic (cold-blooded) animals, monitors must have access to suitable temperatures within these habitats. This is not a problem for monitors living in open habitats, as they can bask in the sunshine to raise their body temperature. However, those species that inhabit closed-canopy forests depend on suitably warm ambient temperatures.

Natural Diet

Monitor lizards are opportunistic predators that consume a variety of different prey items. The number of recorded prey species among all living monitors is undoubtedly in the hundreds.

Smaller specimens and species usually prey on insects, arachnids, reptiles and eggs. Larger species prey primarily on rodents, lizards, snakes and birds, but Komodo dragons take prey as large as pigs, deer and buffalo.

Some species have adapted to a relatively narrow diet, although few specimens of any species are reluctant to turn down available prey. For example, Savannah monitors predate heavily upon snails as adults. Brown rough-necked monitors are thought to predate heavily on crabs.

Many monitors predate upon smaller monitor species and smaller specimens of their own species.

Natural Predators

Monitor lizards have a wide range of predators, which varies from one species and habitat to the next. Nonetheless, a few predator classes are probably especially important to the group as a whole.

Predatory birds, such as hawks, kites and secretary birds, are important predators of young monitors – particularly those that inhabit open habitats.

Dogs, cats and other mammalian predators prey on lizards from time to time. Snakes prey on small monitor lizards, but the tables are often turned, as many monitor lizards are apparently immune to the venom of some snakes.

Nevertheless, the most significant predator of many monitor lizards is other, larger monitor lizards.

In the deserts of Australia, up to seven different monitor species may inhabit the same area. In these areas, the smallest species –

such as rusty and line-tailed goannas – feed on insects and small lizards. (Pianka, Notes on the Biology of Varanus eremius) Freckled goannas and other species predate upon these smaller monitors, while yellow-spotted goannas predate on all of the aforementioned species. Nevertheless, even the large yellow-spotted goannas must be careful of the largest Australian monitors, the Perentie goannas, which readily consume any lizards they encounter. (PIANKA, 2006)

White-throated monitors inhabit scrub and savannah habitats throughout southern and eastern Africa.

Finally, humans are an important predator of monitor lizards. Along with the thousands they catch for food annually, humans harvest thousands more for the leather industry and pet trade.

Chapter 5: Monitor Lizards as Pets

Monitor lizards can make excellent and rewarding pets, but they are completely inappropriate for those unwilling to learn the needs and care requirements of these incredible lizards.

Understanding the Commitment
You will be responsible for your monitor's well-being for the rest of its life. This is important to understand, as monitors may live to be 20 years of age or more. Can you be sure that you will still want to care for your pet in 15 or 20 years?

It is not your lizard's fault if your interests change. Neglecting your pet is wrong, and in some locations, a criminal offense. You must never neglect your monitor, even once the novelty has worn off, and it is no longer fun to clean the cage.

Once you purchase a monitor lizard, its well-being becomes your responsibility until it passes away at the end of a long life, or you have found someone who will agree to take over the care of the animal for you. Understand that it may be very difficult to find someone who will adopt it for you.

Never release pet reptiles into the wild.

Monitor lizards that colonize places outside their native range can cause a variety of harmful effects on the ecosystem

Additionally, escaped reptiles cause a great deal of distress to those who are frightened by them. This leads many local municipalities to adopt pet restrictions or ban reptile keeping entirely.

While the chances of an escaped or released monitor lizard harming anyone are very low, it is unlikely that those who do not enjoy the company of reptiles will see the threat as minor.

The Costs of Captivity
Keeping a monitor lizard is much less expensive than many other pets; however, novices frequently fail to consider the total costs

of purchasing the animal, its habitat, food and other supplies. In addition to the up-front costs, there are on-going costs as well.

Startup Costs

One surprising fact for most new keepers is that the enclosure and equipment often costs more than the animal does (this is not always the case with high-priced species).

Prices fluctuate from one market to the next, but in general, the least you will spend on a monitor lizard is about $50 (£32). The least you will spend on the *initial* habitat and assorted equipment will be about $150 (£95).

Examine the charts on the following pages to get an idea of three different pricing scenarios. While the specific prices listed will vary based on numerous variables, the charts are instructive for first-time buyers.

The first scenario details a keeper who is trying to spend as little as possible, while the second provides a middle-of-the-road example. The third example is of a more extravagant shopper, who wants an expensive monitor, and top-notch equipment.

These charts do not cover all of the costs necessary at startup, such as the initial veterinary visit or shipping charges for the monitor. These charts also fail to allocate anything decorative items.

Inexpensive Option

Savannah Monitor	$50 (£32)
Plastic Storage Box	$40 (£25)
Screen and Hardware for Lid	$10 (£6)
Heat Lamp Fixture and Bulbs	$20 (£13)
Digital Indoor-Outdoor Thermometer	$15 (£9)
Infrared Thermometer	$35 (£22)
Substrate	$10 (£6)
Water Dish, Forceps, Spray Bottles, Misc.	$25 (£16)
Total	**$205 (£129)**

Moderate Option

Spiny-Tailed Monitor	$200 (£126)
Cattle Trough	$75 (£47)
Custom Built Lid	$25 (£16)
Heat Lamp Fixture and Bulbs	$20 (£13)
Digital Indoor-Outdoor Thermometer	$15 (£9)
Infrared Thermometer	$35 (£22)
Substrate	$30 (£19)
Water Dish, Forceps, Spray Bottles, Misc.	$25 (£16)
Total	**$425 (£268)**

Premium Option

Green Tree Monitor	$700 (£443)
Commercial Cage	$500 (£316)
Radiant Heat Panel	$75 (£47)
Thermostat	$50 (£32)
Digital Indoor-Outdoor Thermometer	$15 (£9)
Infrared Thermometer	$35 (£22)
Substrate	$30 (£19)
Water Dish, Forceps, Spray Bottles, Misc.	$25 (£16)
Total	**$1430 (£904)**

Ongoing Costs

Once you have your monitor and his habitat, you must still be able to afford regular care and maintenance. While lizards are low-cost pets, this must be viewed in context.

Compared to a 100-pound Labrador retriever, a monitor lizard is relatively inexpensive. However, when compared to a goldfish, tarantula or hermit crab, monitors are fantastically expensive.

Here is an example of the ongoing costs a typical lizard keeper must endure. Remember: Emergencies can and will happen. You must have some way to weather these storms, and afford a sudden veterinary bill, or the cost to replace a cage that breaks unexpectedly.

The three primary ongoing costs for monitors are:

- **Veterinary Costs**

  While experienced keepers may be able to avoid going to the vet for regular examinations, novices should visit their veterinarian at least once every year. Assuming your lizard is healthy, you may only need to pay for an office visit. However, if your vet sees signs of illness, you may find yourself paying for cultures, medications or procedures. Wise keepers budget at least $200 to $300 (£117 to £175) for veterinary costs each year.

- **Food Costs**

  Food is the single greatest ongoing cost you will experience while caring for your monitor. To obtain a reasonable estimate of your yearly food costs, you must consider the number of meals you will feed your pet per year and the cost of each meal.

  Most monitors should be fed 4 to 6 times per week. Small lizards may require one or two dozen crickets per meal, while larger lizards may require multiple rats at each meal.

Crickets are usually a few cents each, while large rats may cost up to $9 each, you do not purchase them in bulk.

Accordingly, while you may be able to feed a small monitor lizard with a $600 to $700 annual budget, a gigantic monitor lizard may require several thousand dollars of food each year.

- **Maintenance Costs**
It is important to plan for routine and unexpected maintenance costs. Commonly used items, such as paper towels, disinfectant and top soil are rather easy to calculate. However, it is not easy to know how many burned out light bulbs, cracked water dishes or faulty thermostats you will have to replace in a given year.

Those who keep a small monitor in a simple enclosure will find that about $50 (£29) covers their yearly maintenance costs. By contrast, those keeping large monitors in elaborate habitats may spend $200 (£117) or more each year.

Always try to purchase frequently used supplies, such as light bulbs, paper towels and disinfectants in bulk to maximize your savings. It is often beneficial to consult with local reptile-keeping clubs, who often use their members combined needs to make purchases in bulk.

Myths and Misunderstandings

Myth: Monitor lizards need friends or they will get lonely.

Fact: While a few large species, such as Komodo dragons and water monitors, often congregate around carcasses, most monitor lizards are solitary animals that spend the bulk of their lives alone. In fact, monitor lizards may harm or kill each other; males may become especially antagonistic during breeding cycles. House your monitor lizard by himself, unless you intend to breed the species.

Myth: Reptiles grow in proportion to the size of their cage and then stop.

Fact: Reptiles do no such thing. Healthy lizards, snakes and turtles grow throughout their lives, although the rate of growth slows with age. Placing them in a small cage in an attempt to stunt their growth is an unthinkably cruel practice, which is more likely to sicken or kill your pet than stunt its growth.

Myth: Monitor lizards must eat live food.

Fact: While monitor primarily hunt live prey in the wild, most consume carrion when the opportunity presents itself. Whenever possible, hobbyists should feed dead prey to their monitors to minimize the suffering of the prey animal and reduce the chances that the lizard will sustain injury. In contrast to rodents and birds, it is usually not practical to feed your lizard dead insects, and the exercise they derive from chasing bugs is good for their health.

Myth: Reptiles have no emotions and do not suffer.

Fact: While monitor lizards have very primitive brains, and do not have emotions comparable to those of higher mammals, they can absolutely suffer. In fact, many authorities consider monitors to be among the most intelligent reptiles in the world, although few empirical studies have been conducted thus far. Always treat reptiles with the same compassion you would offer a dog, cat or horse.

Myth: Monitors prefer elaborately decorated cages that resemble their natural habitat.

Fact: While most lizards do thrive better in complex habitats that offer a variety of hiding and thermoregulatory options, they do not appreciate your aesthetic efforts. Additionally, the foraging activity of your monitor will likely destroy any decorations you incorporate.

Additionally, while monitor lizards require hiding spaces, they do not seem to mind whether this hiding space is in the form of a rock, a rotten log or piece of lumber. As long as the hiding spot is safe and snug, they will utilize it.

Myth: If your monitor lizard is tame, he will never bite.

Fact: Monitor lizards often become tame pets, but you should never act with impunity. Even tame monitors may become frightened or make a feeding mistake. Bites from larger animals (of about 6 feet or more in length) may cause serious injuries, so avoid handling large monitors by yourself. No matter how long you have owned your pet, always practice safe handling.

Acquiring Your Monitor Lizard

Modern reptile enthusiasts can acquire monitor lizards from a variety of sources, each with a different set of pros and cons.

Pet Stores

Pet stores are often the first place many people see monitor lizards, and a common source for many beginning keepers. However, pet stores are not always the best place to purchase a monitor lizard.

The benefits of shopping at a pet store are that they usually have all of the equipment to care for your new lizard, including cages, heating devices and food items. You will usually be able to inspect the lizard up close before purchase. In some cases, you may be able to choose from more than one specimen.

Many pet stores provide health guarantees for a short period, that provides some recourse if your new pet turns out to be ill.

However, pet stores are retail establishments, and as such, you will pay more than you will from a breeder. Pet stores do not often know the pedigree of the animals they sell, nor are they likely to know the lizard's date of birth, or other pertinent information.

The drawbacks to purchasing a monitor lizard from a pet store relate to the amount of expertise and knowledge of the staff. While some pet stores concentrate on reptiles and may have a staff capable of providing them with proper care, many monitor lizards languish while living in pet stores.

It is also worth considering the increased exposure to pathogens that pet store animals endure, given the constant flow of animals through the facility.

Reptile Expos
Reptile expos are often excellent places to acquire new animals. Reptile expos often feature resellers, breeders and retailers in the same room, all selling various types of monitors and other reptiles.

Often, the prices at such events are quite reasonable and you are often able to select from many different lizards. However, if you have a problem, it may be difficult to find the seller after the event is over.

Breeders
Breeders are the best place for most novices to shop for monitor lizards. Breeders generally offer unparalleled information and support after the sale. Additionally, breeders often know the species well, and are better able to help you learn the husbandry techniques for the animal.

The disadvantage of buying from a breeder is that you must often make such purchases from a distance, either by phone or via the internet. Breeders often have the widest selection of monitors, and are often the only place to find rare forms and truly spectacular specimens.

Classified Advertisements
Newspaper and website classified advertisements sometimes include listings for monitor lizards. While individuals, rather than businesses generally post these, they are a viable option to monitor. Often these sales include the monitor lizard and all of the associated equipment, which is convenient for new keepers. However, be careful to avoid purchasing someone else's "problem" (i.e. a sick or aggressive monitor).

Selecting Your Monitor Lizard
Not all monitor lizards are created equally, so it is important to select a quality individual that will give you the best chance of success.

Practically speaking, the most important criterion to consider is the health of the animal. However, the gender, age and personality of the lizard are also important things to consider.

Health Checklist
While it is not possible to do so if you are purchasing your new pet via the internet or from a non-local source, check your monitor lizard thoroughly for signs of injury or illness before purchasing it.

Avoid the temptation to acquire a sick or injured animal in hopes of nursing him back to health. Not only are you likely to incur substantial veterinary costs while treating your new pet, you will likely fail in your attempts to restore the lizard to full health.

Additionally, by purchasing these animals, you incentivize poor husbandry on the part of the retailer. If retailers lose money on sick or injured animals, they will take steps to avoid this eventuality in the future, by acquiring healthier stock in the first place, and providing better care for their charges.

Whenever possible, handle the monitor lizard you intend to purchase, and observe the following features:

- **Observe the monitor's skin**. It should be free of lacerations and other damage. Pay special attention to those areas that frequently sustain damage, such as the tip of the lizard's tail, the toes and the tip of the snout. A small cut or abrasion may be relatively easy to treat, but significant abrasions and cuts are likely to become infected and require significant treatment.

- **Check the lizard's crevices and creases for mites and ticks**. Mites are about the size of a flake of pepper, and they may be black, brown or red. Mites often move about on the lizard, whereas ticks – if attached and feeding – do not move. Avoid purchasing any animal that has either parasite. Additionally, you should avoid purchasing any other animals from this source, as they are likely to harbor parasites as well.

- **Examine the lizard's eyes, ears and nostrils**. The eyes should blink normally, and be free of discharge. The nostrils should be clear and dry – lizards with runny noses or those who blow bubbles are likely to be suffering from a respiratory infection. However, be aware that lizards often get some water in their nostrils while drinking water. This is no cause for concern. The tympanic membrane (eardrum) should be intact and free of parasites or injury.

- **Gently palpate the animal and ensure no lumps or anomalies are apparent**. Lumps in the muscles or abdominal cavity may indicate parasites, abscesses or tumors.

- **Observe the lizard's demeanor**. Healthy lizards flick their tongues, observe objects in their environment and react to stimuli. When active, the lizard should move about, exploring his environment. While you may wish to avoid purchasing an aggressive, defensive or flighty animal, these behaviors do not necessarily indicate a health problem.

- **Check the lizard's vent**. The vent should be clean and free of smeared feces. Smeared feces can indicate parasites or bacterial infections.

- **Check the lizard's appetite**. If possible, ask the retailer to feed the lizard a few crickets or a rodent. A healthy monitor should exhibit a strong food drive and immediately begin feeding. It is possible to satiate a monitor lizard, causing them to refuse offered food; however, practically speaking, this is unlikely to be the case in a retail environment, where few animals receive more food than they need to live.

- **Feel the monitor's hipbones**. Healthy lizards have a layer of fat over their hips, whereas sick or emaciated animals have highly visible, palpable, hips. Young animals do not often have significant fat stores on their hips, as they a lot most of their calories to growth, so consider the lizards age when examining the fat stores.

In some circumstances, it may be permissible for new keepers to purchase a wounded animal. For example, a monitor lizard may lose a few toes or a significant portion of its tail, but still survive and become healthy. However, such animals must exhibit extraordinary vigor and signs that they have completely healed to make the purchase a sound decision.

The Gender
It is difficult to determine the gender of many monitors, so few hobbyists have the opportunity to choose which sex they acquire. Nevertheless, males and females have a few differences relevant to captive care that should be explored. For example, males of most species grow much larger than the females do. This may not be a problem if you are keeping a small species – a few inches are not going to increase the required space significant. However, larger species – such as white-throated or yellow-spotted monitors – may differ enough in size (not to mention biology) that their space requirements do differ significantly.

Accordingly, if space is an issue, females are generally preferable.

However, females can and will deposit eggs, whether they are kept with a male or not. In all probability, the eggs will not hatch, but egg laying is a taxing event for a female. Additionally, problems such as egg binding may occur, necessitating expensive veterinary care.

Males may be much cheaper for some species that are bred with regularity, such as spiny-tailed monitors. This occurs because breeders need more females than they do males – often they desire two, three or four times as many females as males. This leads to a glut of males in the market place, and downward trending prices. For the beginning hobbyist, it simply means that males are usually less expensive.

The Age
In almost all cases, monitor novices should purchase well-started hatchlings, between 1 and 6 months of age. Avoid purchasing hatchlings that are younger than this, as they are less forgiving of husbandry errors.

While you may have success with a yearling or adult specimen of a small species, these larger animals often intimidate new keepers, which is not the best recipe for success. Large monitor lizards are completely inappropriate as a "first monitor."

The Personality
All monitors are individuals that have different personalities. Some are aggressive, while others are timid. Some tolerate handling and interaction, while others meet such attempts with hissing and tail slapping.

It is often difficult to determine the personality of a monitor lizard while briefly examining it at a reptile expo or in a pet store. However, try to select a confident lizard, who explores his environment and seems curious. Try to avoid those who scurry under the substrate when the cage door opens, or the ones who immediately adopt defensive positions and begin hissing.

Nevertheless, you may be able to tame even the most defensive hatchlings with consistent, gentle handling.

Quarantine

Because new animals may have illnesses or parasites that could infect the rest of your collection, it is wise to quarantine any new acquisitions. This means that you should keep the new animal as separated from the rest of your pets as much as possible, until you have ensured that the new animal is healthy.

During the quarantine period, you should keep the new lizard in a simplified habitat, with a paper substrate, water bowl, basking spot and a few hiding places. Keep the temperature and humidity levels at ideal levels. During the quarantine period, visit the veterinarian to ensure the lizard does not have any lurking illnesses. Your veterinarian can also double check to ensure no external parasites are present on your new pet. If possible, have your veterinarian conduct a fecal examination, to ensure the animal does not have any internal parasites.

Always tend to quarantined animals last, to reduce the chances of transmitting pathogens to your healthy animals. Do not wash water bowls or cage furniture with those belonging to your healthy animals. Whenever possible, use completely separate tools for quarantined animals and those that have been in your collection for some time.

Always be sure to wash your hands thoroughly after handling quarantined animals, their cages or their tools. Particularly careful keepers wear a smock or alternative clothing when handling quarantined animals.

Quarantine new acquisitions for a minimum of 30 days; 60 or 90 days is even better. Many zoos and professional breeders maintain 180- or 360-day-long quarantine periods. Most professional breeders and advanced hobbyists maintain their captives in a state of perpetual quarantine. While they may be kept in the same room with other monitors, their dishes, hide boxes and cages are not shared.

Chapter 6: Providing the Captive Habitat

In most respects, providing monitor lizards with a suitable captive habitat entails functionally replicating the various aspects of their wild habitats. In addition to providing an enclosure, you must provide the right thermal environment, appropriate humidity, substrate, and suitable hiding spots.

Enclosure

Providing your monitor lizard with appropriate housing is and essential aspect of captive care. In essence, the habitat you provide to your pet becomes his "world."

In "the old days," those inclined to keep reptiles had few choices with regard to caging. The two primary options were to build a custom cage from scratch or construct a lid to use with a fish aquarium.

By contrast, modern hobbyists have a variety of options from which to choose. In addition to building custom cages or adapting aquaria, dozens of different cage styles are available – each with different pros and cons.

Dimensions

Throughout their lives, monitor lizards need a cage large enough to lay comfortably, access a range of temperatures and get enough room for exercise.

As a general rule, you must provide your monitor with a cage that is at least three times as long as the lizard is and twice as wide as the lizard is. The proper height varies from one species to the next.

In other words, a full-grown water monitor requires a cage measuring 20 feet long and 10 feet wide – totaling 200 square feet of space. This is the size of a bedroom, and most keepers are unable to provide such space for a pet.

By contrast, a cage for a spiny-tailed monitor should be about 6 feet long and 4 feet wide. This is far more realistic for most keepers.

In addition to total space, the layout of the cage is also important – rectangular cages are strongly preferable for a variety of reasons:

- They allow the keeper to establish better thermal gradients.
- Cages with one long direction allow your lizard more room to move.
- If the cage is accessible via front-opening doors, you will not have to reach as far back in a rectangular cage when cleaning, as you will a square cage.

Aquariums

Aquariums are popular choices for small monitors, largely because of their ubiquity. Virtually any pet store that carries monitor lizards also stocks aquariums.

Aquariums can make suitable cages, but they have a number of drawbacks.

- Aquariums (and other glass cages) are hard to clean
- Aquariums are very fragile
- Aquariums do not retain heat very well
- Aquariums require after-market or custom built lids
- Aquariums often develop water spots from repeated mistings

When keepers use aquariums with screened tops, the excess ventilation may cause the tank to dry out rapidly. This can be a challenge for keepers of rainforest species, who are attempting to keep their cages relatively humid. To work around this, some keepers attach plastic or glass covers over a portion of the screened lid.

Another problem with aquariums and glass cages is that they may produce reflections which can startle or stress the monitor lizard. Additionally, because monitor lizards do not encounter transparent materials in the wild, they do not appear to understand glass. This can cause them to rub or press their nose against the glass for extended periods of time, causing injuries.

Spiny-tailed monitors are one of the smaller monitor species, which makes them easier to house.

Commercial Cages

Commercially produced cages have a number of benefits over other enclosures. Commercial cages usually feature doors on the front of the cage, which provide better access than top-opening cages do. Additionally, bypass glass doors or framed, hinged doors are generally more secure than after-market screened lids are.

Manufacturers produce plastic cages in dimensions that make more sense for lizards, and often have features that aid in heating and lighting the cage.

Commercial cages can be made out of wood, metal, glass or other substances, but the majority of commercial cages are made from PVC or ABS plastic.

Commercial cages are available in two primary varieties: those molded from one piece of plastic and those that are assembled from several different sheets. Assembled cages are less expensive and easier to construct, but molded cages have few (if any) seams or cracks in which bacteria and other pathogens can hide.

Some cage manufacturers produce cages in multiple colors. White is probably the best color for novices, as it is easy to see dirt, mites and other small problems. A single mite crawling on a white cage surface is very visible, even from a distance.

Black cages do not show dirt as well. This can be helpful for more experienced keepers who have developed proper hygiene techniques over time. Additionally, many monitor lizards are beautiful when viewed against black cage walls.

Plastic Storage Containers
Plastic storage containers, such as those used for shoes, sweaters or food, make suitable cages for very small or young monitor lizards. However, the lids for plastic storage boxes are rarely secure enough for use without modifications.

Hobbyists and breeders overcome this by incorporating Velcro straps, hardware latches or other strategies into plastic storage container cages.

When plastic containers are used, you must drill or melt numerous holes for air exchange.

Drill or melt all of the holes from the inside of the box, towards the outside of the box. This will help reduce the chances of leaving sharp edges inside the cage, which could cut your pet.

If you intend to heat a single plastic storage box with a heat lamp, you will need to cut a hole in the lid, and cover the hole with hardware cloth or screen. Attach the mesh or hardware cloth with silicone or cable ties. You can now place the heat lamp on top of the mesh.

Homemade Cages
For keepers with access to tools and the desire and skill to use them, it is possible to construct homemade cages.

A number of materials are suitable for cage construction, and each has different pros and cons. Wood is commonly used, but must be adequately sealed to avoid rotting, warping or absorbing offensive odors.

Plastic sheeting is a very good material, but few have the necessary skills, knowledge and tools necessary for cage construction. Additionally, some plastics may have extended off-gassing times.

Glass can be used, whether glued to itself or when used with a frame. Custom-built glass cages can be better than aquariums, as you can design them in dimensions that are appropriate for monitor lizards. Additionally, they can be constructed in such a way that the door is on the front of the cage, rather than the top.

Security and safety are of paramount importance when constructing a custom cage.

Screen Cages
Screen cages make excellent habitats for some lizards and frogs, but they are not suitable for monitors, whose sharp claws can make quick work of the mesh material. Screened cages do not retain heat well, and they are hard to keep suitably humid. Additionally, they are difficult to clean. Screen cages are prone to developing week spots that can give the inhabitant enough of a hole to push through and escape.

Chapter 7: Establishing the Thermal Environment

Providing the proper thermal environment is one of the most important aspects of reptile husbandry. As ectothermic ("cold blooded") animals, monitor lizards rely on the local temperatures to regulate the rate at which their metabolism operates. Providing a proper thermal environment can mean the difference between keeping your pet healthy and spending your time at the veterinarian's office, battling infections and illness.

While there is variation between species, genders and individuals, the preferred body temperature of most active monitor lizards is about 95 to 97 degrees Fahrenheit (35 to 36 degrees Celsius). During the night, the body temperature drops slightly in tropical species, and precipitously in those species from open habitats.

Cages for tropical species should not fall below about 77 degrees Fahrenheit (25 degrees Celsius) at night, while cages containing desert-dwelling species may safely drop into the low 60s Fahrenheit (15 degrees Celsius).

While they may bask at temperatures greatly exceeding this, body temperatures of approximately 105 degrees Fahrenheit (41 degrees Celsius) are fatal for virtually all monitor species.

Thermal Gradients
In the wild, monitor lizards move between different microhabitats so that they can maintain ideal body temperature as much as possible. You want to provide similar opportunities for captive reptiles by creating a thermal gradient.

To establish a thermal gradient, place the heating devices at one end of the habitat. If more than one heat source is required for the habitat, they should be clustered at one end. This creates a basking spot, which should have the highest temperatures in the cage – between 110 and 130 degrees Fahrenheit (43 to 54 degrees Celsius). Some desert dwelling species may even bask at surface temperatures of 140 degrees Fahrenheit (60 degrees Celsius), but temperatures this high are not necessary.

Because there is no heat source at the other end of the cage, the temperature will gradually fall as your monitor moves away from the heat source. Ideally, the cool end of the cage should be in the high 70s Fahrenheit (26 degrees Celsius).

The need to establish a thermal gradient is one of the most compelling reasons to use a large cage. In general, the larger the cage, the easier it is to establish a suitable thermal gradient.

Heat Lamps

Heat lamps are one of the best choices for supplying heat to your monitor lizard. Heat lamps consist of a reflector dome and an incandescent bulb. The light bulb produces heat (in addition to light) and the metal reflector dome directs the heat to a spot inside the cage.

If you use a cage with a metal screen lid, you can rest the reflector dome directly on the screen; otherwise, you will need to clamp the lamp to something over the cage. Always be sure that the lamp is securely attached and will not be dislodged by vibration, children or pets. Always opt to purchase heavy-duty reflector domes with ceramic bases, rather than economy units with plastic bases.

One of the greatest benefits of using heat lamps to maintain the temperature of your pet's habitat is the flexibility. While heat tapes and other devices are easy to adjust, you need a rheostat or thermostat to do so. Such devices are not prohibitively expensive, but they will raise the budget of your lizard's habitat.

By contrast, heat lamps offer flexibility in two ways:

Changing the Bulb Wattage

The simplest way to adjust the temperature of your monitor's cage is by changing the wattage of the bulb you are using.

For example, if a 40-watt light bulb is not raising the temperature of the basking spot high enough, you may try a 60-watt bulb.

Alternatively, if a 100-watt light bulb is elevating the cage temperatures higher than are appropriate, switching to a 60-watt bulb may help.

Adjusting the Height of the Heat Lamp

The closer the heat lamp is to the cage, the warmer the cage will be. If the habitat is too warm, you can raise the light, which should lower the cage temperatures slightly.

However, the higher you raise the lamp, the larger the basking spot becomes. It is important to be careful that you do not raise the light too high, which results in reducing the effectiveness of the cage's thermal gradient. In very large cages, this may not compromise the thermal gradient very much, but in a small cage, it may eliminate the "cool side" of the habitat.

In other words, if your heat lamp creates a basking spot that is roughly 1-foot in diameter when it rests directly on the screen, it may produce a slightly cooler, but larger basking spot when raised 6-inches above the level of the screen.

One way to avoid reducing the effectiveness of the gradient is through the use of "spot" bulbs, which produce a relatively narrow beam of light. Such lights may be slightly more expensive than economy bulbs, but because they make heat gradients easier to achieve, they deserve consideration.

One problem with using heat lamps is that many manufacturers have stopped producing incandescent bulbs. In some municipalities, they may even be illegal to sell. It remains to be seen if incandescent bulbs will remain available to herpetoculturists over the long term or not. Fortunately, many other heating options are available.

Ceramic Heat Emitters

Ceramic heat emitters are small inserts that function as light bulbs do, except that they do not produce any visible light – they only produce heat.

You can use ceramic heat emitters in reflector-dome fixtures, just as you would use a heat lamp. The benefits of such devices are numerous:

- They typically last much longer than light bulbs do
- They are suitable for use with thermostats
- They allow for the creation of overhead basking spots
- They can be used day or night

However, the devices do have three primary drawbacks:

- They are very hot when in operation
- They are much more expensive than light bulbs
- You cannot tell by looking if they are hot or cool. This can be a safety hazard – touching a ceramic heat emitter while it is hot is likely to cause serious burns.

Ceramic heat emitters are much less expensive than radiant heat panels are. This causes many to select them instead of radiant heat panels. However, radiant heat panels are generally preferable to ceramic heat emitters, as they usually have a light that indicates when they are on, and they do not get as hot on the surface.

Radiant Heat Panels

Quality radiant heat panels are excellent choices for heating most reptile habitats, including those containing monitor lizards. Radiant heat panels are essentially heat pads that stick to the roof of the habitat. They usually feature rugged, plastic or metal casings and internal reflectors to direct the infrared heat back into the cage.

Radiant heat panels have a number of benefits over traditional heat lamps and under tank heat pads:

- They do not contact the animal at all, thus reducing the risk of burns.
- They do not produce visible light, which means they are useful for both diurnal and nocturnal heat production. They can be used in conjunction with fluorescent light fixtures during the day, and remain on at night once the lights go off.

- They are inherently flexible. Unlike many devices that do not work well with pulse-proportional thermostats, most radiant heat panels work well with on-off and pulse-proportional thermostats.

The only real drawback to radiant heat panels is their cost: radiant heat panels often cost about two to three times the price of light- or heat pad-oriented systems. However, many radiant heat panels outlast light bulbs and heat pads – a fact which offsets their high initial cost.

Heat Pads

Heat pads are an attractive option for many new keepers, but they are not without drawbacks.

- Heat pads have a high risk for causing contact burns.
- If they malfunction, they can damage the cage as well as the surface on which they are placed.
- They are more likely to cause a fire than heat lamps or radiant heat panels are.
- They are not ideal for arboreal species.

However, if installed properly (which includes allowing fresh air to flow over the exposed side of the heat pad) and used in conjunction with a thermostat, they can be reasonably safe. With heat pads, it behooves the keeper to purchase premium products, despite the small increase in price.

Heat Tape

Heat tape is somewhat akin to "stripped down" heat pads. In fact, most heat pads are simply pieces of heat tape that have already been connected and sealed inside a plastic envelope.

Heat tape is primarily used to heat large numbers of cages simultaneously. It is generally inappropriate for novices, and requires the keeper to make electrical connections. Additionally, a thermostat is always required when using heat tape.

Historically, homeowners used heat tape to keep water pipes from freezing – not to heat reptile cages. While some manufacturers design commercial heat tapes specifically for reptiles, many have not. Accordingly, it may be illegal, not to mention dangerous, to use heat tapes for purposes other than for which they are designed.

Heat Cables

Heat cables are similar to heat tape, in that they heat a long strip of the cage, but they are much more flexible and easy to use. Many heat cables are suitable to use inside the cage, while others are designed for use outside the habitat.

Always be sure to purchase heat cables that are designed to be used in reptile cages. Those sold at hardware stores are not appropriate for use in a cage.

Heat cables must be used in conjunction with a thermostat, or, at the very least, a rheostat.

Hot Rocks

In the early days of commercial reptile products, faux rocks, branches and caves with internal heating elements were very popular. However, they have generally fallen out of favor among modern keepers. These rocks and branches were often made with poor craftsmanship and cheap materials, causing them to fail and produce tragic results. Additionally, many keepers used the rocks improperly, leading to injuries, illnesses and death for many unfortunate reptiles.

These types of heat sources are not designed to heat an entire cage; they are designed to provide a localized source of heat for the reptile. Nevertheless, many keepers tried to use them as the primary heat source for the cage, resulting in dangerously cool cage temperatures.

When reptiles must rely on small, localized heat sources placed in otherwise chilly cages, they often hug these heat sources for extended periods of time. This can lead to serious thermal burns – whether or not the units function properly. This illustrates the key reason why these devices make adequate supplemental heat sources, but they are not suitable as the primary heat source for a cage.

Modern hot rocks and branches utilize better features, materials and craftsmanship than the old models did, but they still offer few benefits to the keeper or the kept. Additionally, any heating devices that are designed to be used inside the cage necessitate passing an electric cable through a hole, which is not always easy to accomplish. However, some cages do feature passageways for chords.

Thermometers

It is important to monitor the cage temperatures very carefully to ensure your pet stays health. Just as a water test kit is an aquarist's best friend, a quality thermometer is one of the most important husbandry tools for reptiles.

Ambient and Surface Temperatures

Two different types of temperature are relevant for pet lizards: ambient temperatures and surface temperatures.

The ambient temperature in your animal's cage is the air temperature. By contrast, surface temperatures are the temperatures of the objects in the cage.

For example, the air temperatures may be 90 degrees Fahrenheit (32 degrees Celsius) on a hot summer day. However, the surface of a black rock may be much hotter than this. If you checked the surface temperatures of the rock, it may be in excess of 120 degrees Fahrenheit (48 degrees Celsius).

In general, the ambient temperatures require more frequent monitoring and attention. As long as the surface temperatures of the cage do not exceed about 130 degrees Fahrenheit, your pet is not likely to be harmed from incidental contact. However, ambient temperatures of 130 degrees would be fatal very quickly.

Measure the cage's ambient temperatures with a digital thermometer. An indoor-outdoor model will feature a probe that allows you to measure the temperature at both ends of the thermal gradient at once. For example, you may position the thermometer at the cool side of the cage, but place the remote probe under the basking lamp.

Standard digital thermometers do not measure surface temperatures well. Instead, you should use a non-contact, infrared thermometer. Such devices will allow you to measure surface temperatures accurately and from a short distance away.

Thermostats and Rheostats

Some heating devices, such as heat lamps, are designed to operate at full capacity for the entire time that they are turned on. Such devices should not be used with thermostats – instead, care should be taken to calibrate the proper temperature by tweaking the bulb wattage.

Other devices, such as heat pads, heat tape and radiant heat panels are designed to be used with a regulating device, such as a thermostat or rheostat, which maintains the proper temperature

Rheostats

Rheostats are similar to light-dimmer switches, and they allow you to reduce the output of a heating device. In this way, you can dial in the proper temperature for the habitat.

The drawback to rheostats is that they only regulate the amount of power going to the device – they do not monitor the cage temperature or adjust the power flow automatically. In practice, even with the same level of power entering the device, the amount of heat generated by most heat sources will vary over the course of the day.

If you set the rheostat so that it keeps the cage at the right temperature in the morning, it may become too hot by the middle of the day. Conversely, setting the proper temperature during the middle of the day may leave the morning temperatures too cool.

Care must be taken to ensure that the rheostat controller is not inadvertently bumped or jostled, causing the temperature to rise or fall outside of healthy parameters.

Thermostats

Thermostats are similar to rheostats, except that they also feature a temperature probe that monitors the temperature in the cage (or under the basking source). This allows the thermostat to adjust the power going to the device as necessary to maintain a predetermined temperature.

For example, if you place the temperature probe under a basking spot powered by a radiant heat panel, the thermostat will keep the temperature relatively constant under the basking site.

There are two different types of thermostats:

- On-Off Thermostats work by cutting the power to the device when the probe's temperature reaches a given temperature. For example, if the thermostat were set to 85 degrees Fahrenheit (29 degrees Celsius), the heating device would turn off whenever the temperature exceeds this threshold. When the temperature falls below 85, the thermostat restores power to the unit, and the heater begins functioning again. This cycle will continue to repeat, thus maintaining the temperature within a relatively small range.

  Be aware that on-off thermostats have a "lag" factor, meaning that they do not turn off when the temperature reaches a given temperature. They turn off when the temperature is a few degrees *above* that temperature, and then turn back on when the temperate is a little *below* the set point. Because of this, it is important to avoid setting the temperature at the limits of your pet's acceptable range. Some premium models have an adjustable amount of threshold for this factor, which is helpful.

- Pulse proportional thermostats work by constantly sending pulses of electricity to the heater. By varying the rate of pulses, the amount of energy reaching the heating devices varies. A small computer inside the thermostat adjusts this rate to match the set-point temperature as measured by the probe. Accordingly, pulse proportional thermostats maintain much more consistent temperatures than on-off thermostats do.

Lights should not be used with thermostats, as the constant flickering may stress your pet. Conversely, heat pads, heat tape, radiant heat panels and ceramic heat emitters should always be used with either a rheostat or, preferably, a thermostat to avoid overheating your monitor lizard.

Thermostat Failure

If used for long enough, all thermostats eventually fail. The question is will yours fail today or twenty years from now. While some thermostats fail in the "off" position, a thermostat that fails in the "on" position may overheat your lizards. Unfortunately, tales of entire collections being lost to a faulty thermostat are too common.

Accordingly, it behooves the keeper to acquire high-quality thermostats. Some keepers use two thermostats, connected in series arrangement. By setting the second thermostat (the "backup thermostat") a few degrees higher than the setting used on the "primary thermostat," you safeguard yourself against the failure of either unit.

In such a scenario, the backup thermostat allows the full power coming to it to travel through to the heating device, as the temperature never reaches its higher set-point temperature.

However, if the first unit fails in the "on" position, the second thermostat will keep the temperatures from rising too high. The temperature will rise a few degrees in accordance with the higher set-point temperature, but it will not get hot enough to harm your pets.

If the backup thermostat fails in the "on" position, the first thermostat retains control. If either fails in the "off" position, the temperature will fall until you rectify the situation, but a brief exposure to relatively cool temperatures is unlikely to be fatal.

Nighttime Heating

In most circumstances, you should provide your monitor lizard with a minor temperature drop at night. Some keepers have success by providing constant heat, but wild monitor lizards experience day-night temperature fluctuations, which may provide some benefits.

If you keep desert-dwelling species, you can probably just turn the heating devices off at night; however, cages housing rainforest species should not be allowed to drop lower than the high 70s at night. This may require you to install secondary, nighttime heating devices to provide suitable heat at night.

You can plug the heating devices (and thermostats or rheostats) into a lamp-timer to automate the process. Some thermostats even have features that adjust the temperature of the thermostat during the night, lowering it to a specified level.

Others, who must provide some type of nocturnal heat source for their pet, can do so in a number of ways. Virtually any non-light-emitting heat source will function adequately in this capacity. Ceramic heating elements, radiant heat panels and heat pads, cables and tape all work well for supplying nocturnal heat.

Red lights can be used in reflector domes to provide heat as well. In fact, red lights can be used for heating during the day and night, but the cage will not be illuminated very well, unless other lights are incorporated during the day.

Incorporating Thermal Mass

One underutilized technique that is helpful for raising the temperature of a cage is to increase the cage's thermal mass.

Rocks, large water dishes and ceramic cage decorations are examples of items that may work in such contexts. These objects will absorb heat from the heat source, and then re-radiate heat into the habitat.

This changes the thermal characteristics of the habitat greatly. Often, keepers in cool climates benefit from these techniques when trying to warm cages sufficiently. By simply adding a large rock, the cage may eventually warm up a few degrees.

Raising the cage's thermal mass also helps to reduce the cage's rate of cooling in the evening. By placing a thick rock under the basking light, it will absorb heat all day and radiate this heat after the lights turn off. Eventually it will reach room temperature, but this may take hours.

Always remember to monitor the cage surface temperatures and ambient temperatures regularly after changing the thermal characteristics of the cage. Pay special attention to the surface temperatures of items placed on or under a heat source.

Experiment with different amounts of thermal mass in the cage. Use items of different sizes, shapes and materials, and see how the cage temperatures change. In general, the more thermal mass in the cage, the more constant the temperature will stay.

Chapter 8: Lighting the Enclosure

Monitor lizards may become seriously ill if they do not have access to appropriate lighting. Learning how to provide the proper lighting for reptiles is sometimes an arduous task for beginners, but it is very important to the long-term health of your pet that you do. To understand the type of light your lizard needs, and understand how to acquire the right type, you must first understand a little bit about light. Light is a type of energy that physicists call electromagnetic radiation; it travels in waves. These waves may differ in amplitude, which correlates to the vertical distance between consecutive wave crests and troughs, frequency, which correlates with the number of crests per unit of time, and wavelength. Wavelength is the distance from one crest to the next, or one trough to the next. Wavelength and frequency are inversely proportional, meaning that as the wavelength increases, the frequency decreases. It is more common for reptile keepers to discuss wavelengths rather than frequencies.

The sun produces energy (light) with a very wide range of constituent wavelengths. Some of these wavelengths fall within a range called the visible spectrum; humans can detect these rays with their eyes. Such waves have wavelengths between about 390 and 700 nanometers. Rays with wavelengths longer or shorter than these limits are broken into their own groups and given different names. Those rays with around 390 nanometer wavelengths or less are called ultraviolet rays or UV rays. UV rays are broken down into three different categories, just as the different colors correspond with different wavelengths of visible light. UVA rays have wavelengths between 315 to 400 nanometers, while UVB rays have wavelengths between 280 and 315 nanometers while UVC rays have wavelengths between 100 and 280 nanometers. Rays with wavelengths of less than 280 nanometers are called x-rays and gamma rays. While at the other end of the visible spectrum, infrared rays have wavelengths longer than 700 nanometers, while microwaves and radio waves are even longer.

UVA rays are important for food recognition, appetite, activity and eliciting natural behaviors. UVB rays are necessary for many reptiles to produce vitamin D3. Without this vitamin, reptiles cannot properly metabolize their calcium.

The light that comes from the sun and light bulbs is composed of a combination of wavelengths, which create the blended white light that you perceive. This combination of wavelengths varies slightly from one light source to the next. The sun produces very balanced white light, while "economy" incandescent bulbs produce relatively fewer blue rays and yields a yellow-looking light. High-quality bulbs designed for reptiles often produce very balanced, white light. The degree to which light causes objects to look as they would under sunlight is called the Color Rendering Index, or CRI. Sunlight has a CRI of 100, while quality bulbs have CRIs of 80 to 90; by contrast, a typical incandescent bulb has a CRI of 40 to 50

Another important characteristic of light that relates to monitor lizards is luminosity, or the brightness of light. Measured in units called Lux, luminosity is an important consideration for your lighting system. While you cannot possibly replicate the intensity of the sun's light, it is desirable in most circumstances to ensure the habitat is lit as well as is reasonably possible. For example, in the tropics, the sunlight intensity averages around 100,000 Lux at midday; by comparison, the lights in a typical family living room only produce about 50 Lux.

Without bright lighting, many reptiles become lethargic, depressed or exhibit hibernating behaviors. Dim lighting may inhibit feeding and cause monitors to become stressed and ill. However, it is important to distinguish between forest-dwelling species, such as green tree monitors, from open-habitat species, such as yellow-spotted monitors. Forests – especially closed canopy rainforests – are relatively dim environments, whereas open plains and deserts are incredibly bright. In practice, you should tailor the light levels to match those of your lizard's natural habitat. However, it is better to err on the side of too bright, rather than too dim. To summarize, monitor lizards require:

- Light of the appropriate intensity
- Light that is comprised of a significant amount of UVA and UVB radiation
- Light with a high color-rendering index

Now that you know what monitor lizards require, you can go about designing the lighting system for the habitat. Ultraviolet radiation is the most difficult component of proper lighting to provide, so it makes sense to begin by examining the types of bulbs that produce UV radiation.

The only commercially produced bulbs that produce significant amounts of UVA and UVB and suitable for a monitor habitat are linear fluorescent light bulbs, compact fluorescent light bulbs and mercury vapor bulbs. While lighting and heating are separate needs, some bulbs produce both heat and light, while others only produce light (and an insignificant amount of heat).

Neither type of fluorescent bulb produces significant amounts of heat, but mercury vapor bulbs produce a lot of heat and serve a dual function. In many cases, keepers elect to use both types of lights – a mercury vapor bulb for a warm basking site with high levels of UV radiation and fluorescent bulbs to light the rest of the cage without raising the temperature. You can also use fluorescent bulbs to provide the requisite UV radiation and use a regular incandescent bulb to generate the basking spot.

Fluorescent bulbs have a much longer history of use than mercury vapor bulbs, which makes some keepers more comfortable using them. However, many models only produce moderate amounts of UVB radiation. While some mercury vapor bulbs produce significant quantities of UVB, some question the wisdom of producing more UV radiation than the animal receives in the wild. Additionally, mercury vapor bulbs are much too powerful to use in small habitats, and they are more expensive initially.

Most fluorescent bulbs must be placed within 12 inches of the basking surface, while some mercury vapor bulbs should be placed farther away from the basking surface – be sure to read the manufacturer's instructions before use. Be sure that the bulbs you purchase specifically state the amount of UVB radiation they produce; this figure is expressed as a percentage, for example 7% UVB. Most UVB-producing bulbs require replacement every six to 12 months – whether or not they have stopped producing light. However, ultraviolet radiation is only one of the characteristics that lizard keepers must consider. The light bulbs used must also produce a sunlight-like spectrum. Fortunately, most high-quality light bulbs that produce significant amounts of UVA and UVB radiation also feature a high color-rendering index. The higher the CRI, the better, but any bulbs with a CRI of 90 or above will work well. If you are having trouble deciding between two otherwise evenly matched bulbs, select the one with the higher CRI value.

Brightness is the final, and easiest, consideration for the keeper to address. While no one yet knows what the ideal luminosity for a monitor lizard's cage, keepers of desert species should strive to create very brightly lit enclosures; keepers of forest-dwelling species should provide very bright basking spots, but the rest of the cage should be somewhat dimmer. Sometimes, a single mercury vapor bulb will fail to illuminate the enclosure properly, while two mercury vapor bulbs make the habitat much too hot.

It may be necessary to use a combination of linear or compact fluorescent light bulbs along with mercury vapor bulbs to raise the luminosity to a desired level. To err on the side of caution, install high quality, UVA- and UVB-producing bulbs with a high CRI value over two-thirds of the cage so that most of the cage is well lit, but your lizard can still retreat to shade if he desires.

Connect the lights to an electric timer to keep the length of the day and night consistent. For equatorial species, it is appropriate to keep the lights on for 12 hours; however, species that live farther from the equator should have fluctuating seasonal light cycles. For example, the lights may be on for 10 hours per day in the winter, 11 hours per day in the spring and fall and 12 hours per day in the summer.

Chapter 9: Substrate and Furniture

Once you have acquired your enclosure, you must place appropriate items inside to provide your lizard with a suitable habitat. In general, these items take the form of an appropriate substrate and proper cage furniture.

Substrate

Substrates give your lizard a comfortable surface on which to rest and crawl, and they absorb any liquids present. Additionally, many monitor lizards spend lots of time digging for food and create burrows for themselves.

There are a variety of acceptable choices, all of which have benefits and drawbacks.

Soils

The best substrate for most monitor lizards is some type of soil. You can make a suitable soil substrate by digging up your own soil, purchasing organic soil products or mixing your own blend.

Tropical, arboreal species do not require a substrate suitable for burrowing, but most other monitors need soil that will allow a burrow to form.

Experiment with different materials to devise a good mix. Organic topsoil, mulch, leaf litter, sand and decomposed granite are all potential ingredients for your custom blend.

Ideally, the soil should form a suitable burrow, yet still be easy to spot clean. Avoid substrates that create excessive dust.

Cypress Mulch

Cypress mulch is a popular substrate choice for many tropical species. It looks attractive and holds humidity well. However, some brands (or individual bags among otherwise good brands) produce a stick-like mulch, rather than mulch composed of thicker pieces.

These sharp sticks can injure the keeper and the kept. It usually only takes one cypress mulch splinter jammed under a keeper's fingernail to cause them to switch substrates.

Cypress mulch does not allow monitors to construct proper burrows, but many species will dig down into the mulch to hide. Cypress mulch is best suited as a substrate for arboreal, tropical species, such as green tree monitors and Timor monitors.

Fir (Orchid) Bark
The bark of fir trees is often used for orchid propagation, and so it is often called "orchid bark." Orchid bark is very attractive, though not quite as natural looking as pine bark. However, it exceeds pine in most other ways except cost.

Orchid bark absorbs water very well, so keepers who maintain rainforest species often use it. Additionally, orchid bark is easy to spot clean. However, monthly replacement can be expensive for those living in the Eastern United States and Europe.

Pine
Pine shavings are similar to aspen shavings. Besides being unsuitable for humid cages, pine shavings are very aromatic. Some keepers worry that the fumes from pine shavings may be toxic to reptiles. While this has yet to be conclusively demonstrated, it is quite possible. The best course of action is to err on the side of caution, and avoid pine shavings.

By contrast, pine bark mulch is a reasonable substrate for tropical monitors. The bark from pine trees is not particularly aromatic and contains no sap. Additionally, pine bark mulch resists decay for longer than mulch made from the wood of the trees, although it eventually does breakdown in damp conditions.

Paper Products
Newspaper and similar substrates are acceptable for temporary, quarantine cages, but these types of substrates do not afford monitors sufficient traction and the sheets quickly become shredded from the monitor's claws.

Aspen
Shredded aspen bark is a popular substrate choice for many reptiles, but it is not ideal for monitor lizards. Aspen decomposes rapidly when it gets wet, and it is not a good substrate for high-humidity cages. Monitor lizards frequently ingest portions of their substrate when they are eating, and they may become impacted from ingesting aspen fibers.

Substrates to Avoid
Some substrates are completely inappropriate for monitor lizard maintenance, and should be avoided at all costs. These include:

- **Cedar Shavings** – Cedar shavings produce toxic fumes that may sicken or kill your monitor. Always avoid cedar shavings.

- **Sand** – Sand is too abrasive and desiccating for most monitor lizards, and it does not allow the establishment of burrows.

- **Gravel** – Gravel is difficult to clean and heavy. It does not allow the monitors to produce a burrow, and the lizards may swallow some of the rocks, which can be life-threatening.

- **Artificial Turf** – Artificial turf is completely inappropriate for monitor lizards. In addition to preventing the lizards from creating burrows, the threads often come loose from the turf. These threads can wrap around the lizard's toes or tail tip and cause serious injuries. These threads may also be swallowed by the lizard, leading to obstructions.

- **Linoleum or Tile** – Although tile and linoleum make suitable substrates for some reptiles, they are not appropriate for monitor lizards. In addition to preventing the lizard from burrowing, these substrates do not provide the lizards with traction or absorb expelled liquids.

Substrate Comparison Chart

Substrate	Pros	Cons
Soil	Allows burrowing, easy to spot clean, usually affordable (sometimes free).	Requires experimentation to devise suitable mix.
Cypress Mulch	Attractive and easy to spot clean. Retains moisture well. May support burrows for small lizards.	May be ingested, messy, can be expensive. Does not allow for burrow formation for large lizards.
Fir (Orchid) Bark	Attractive and easy to spot clean. Retains moisture well.	May be ingested, messy, can be expensive. Does not allow for burrow formation.
Pine Bark Mulch	Attractive and easy to spot clean.	May be ingested, messy, can be expensive. Does not allow for burrow formation.
Newspaper	Safe, low-cost, and easy to maintain substrate for temporary or quarantine cages.	Unsuitable for long term use. Does not allow burrowing or provide traction.
Commercial Paper Product	Safe and easy to maintain substrate for temporary or quarantine cages.	Unsuitable for long term use. Does not allow burrowing or provide traction.
Aspen Shavings	Easy to spot clean. If compressed, small lizards may be able to construct burrows.	Rots when wet, dusty and expensive.

Cage Furniture

Different monitor lizard species require different types of cage furniture. Tropical, tree-dwellers need plenty of branches and other objects to climb, while desert dwelling burrowers need plenty of space, and only want a few hiding places and basking platforms. Additionally, some species inhabit rocky outcroppings and require stable rock piles for basking and foraging.

In all cases, the cage furniture used should be as simple as possible, to facilitate maintenance. Additionally, only use furniture robust enough to withstand your lizard's activity.

You can use natural materials, such as stones and branches, you can purchase commercial cage props (although they are seldom offered in sizes large enough to be appropriate for large monitors) or you can make your own furniture.

Aside from those that serve a purely aesthetic purpose, cage furniture comes in two primary forms, relevant to monitor lizards: climbing branches and hiding spots.

Insects make up a majority of the diet of small monitors.

Branches
Climbing branches are an important component of some monitor cages. Many species climb trees (or other structures) to escape predators, forage for food or to reach suitable basking locations. Accordingly, it is advisable to provide such species with climbing branches or perches.

The branches should be larger in diameter than your monitor lizard, and attached securely to ensure that they will not fall and injure your pet.

Some of the common species that should always have climbing branches in their cages include:

- All climbing members of the *Euprepiosaurus* subgenus, including green, blue and black tree monitors
- All members of the African subgenus *Polydaedalus* – particularly while the lizards are young
- Brown rough-necked and black rough-necked monitors
- Crocodile monitors
- Water monitors
- Tree climbing dwarf monitors, such as freckled and mournful goannas

Acquiring and Preparing Perches
You can purchase climbing branches from pet and craft stores, or you can collect them yourself. When collecting your own branches, try to use branches that are still attached to trees (always obtain permission first). Such branches are less likely to harbor insects or other invertebrate pests than fallen, dead branches will.

Most of the insects that infest wood will cause your lizard no harm, but they may scatter frass (insect droppings mixed with wood shavings) throughout the cage, causing the keeper more work. Theoretically, some of these insects may be damaging to your house, should they escape the cage.

It is always advisable to sterilize branches before placing them in a cage. The easiest way to do so is by placing the branch in a 300-degree oven for about 15 minutes. Doing so should kill the vast majority of pests and pathogens lurking inside the wood.

Some keepers like to cover their branches with a water-sealing product. This is acceptable if a non-toxic product is used and the branches are allowed to air dry for several days before being placed in the cage. However, as branches are relatively easy and inexpensive to replace, it is not necessary to seal them if you plan to replace them.

Attaching Perches to the Enclosure
You can attach the branches to the cage walls in many different ways. The branches should attach very securely to the cage, but you must be able to remove them when necessary.

You can use hooks and eye-screws to suspend branches, which allows for quick and easy removal, but it is only applicable for cages with walls that will accept and support the eye-screws.

It can be challenging to suspend branches in glass or metal cages. It is often necessary to use an adhesive to hold the supports securely to the cage walls. This can be a problem if the adhesive loses strength and fails with your lizard on top of it.

Another option is to make self-supporting structures for your monitor to climb. Many branches can be placed in cages in such a way that they will support themselves. Use complex branches and trim them to fit the glass habitat. Usually, a large part of the branch should be on the cage floor to support its weight. Be careful placing pressure on glass walls or panels, as they crack easily.

Many different types of branches can be used in monitor lizard cages. Most non-aromatic hardwoods suffice. See the chart below for specific recommendations.

Whenever collecting wood to be used as cage props, bring a ruler so that you can visualize how large the branch will be, once it is back in the cage. Leave several inches of spare material at each end of the branch; this way, you can cut the perch to the correct length, once you arrive back home.

Always wash branches with plenty of hot water and a stiff, metal-bristled scrub brush to remove as much dirt, dust and fungus as possible before placing them in your monitor's cage. Clean stubborn spots with a little bit of dish soap, but be sure to rinse them thoroughly afterwards.

Recommended Tree Species for Perches

Recommended Species	Species to Avoid
Maple trees (*Acer* spp.)	Cherry trees (*Prunus* spp.)
Oak trees (*Quercus* spp.)	Pine trees (*Pinus* spp.)
Walnut trees (*Juglans* spp.)	Cedar trees (*Cedrus* spp., etc.)
Ash trees (*Fraxinus* spp.)	Juniper trees (*Juniperus* spp.)
Dogwood trees (*Cornus* spp.)	Poison ivy / oak (*Toxicodendron* spp.)
Sweetgum trees (*Liquidambar stryaciflua*)	
Crepe Myrtle trees (*Lagerstroemia* spp.)	
Tuliptrees (*Liriodendron tulipifera*)	
Pear trees (*Pyrus* spp.)	
Apple trees (*Malus* spp.)	
Manzanitas (*Arctostaphylos* spp.)	
Grapevine (*Vitis* spp.)	

Rock Piles

Rock piles should be very stable and provide basking opportunities for the lizards. You can use virtually any type of rock you like, but avoid those with excessively rough texture or sharp edges.

Consider cementing the rocks into place, but you must weigh the additional safety against the increased labor that will be necessary to tend to a massive structure, rather than several individual rocks.

If you would rather make faux rocks, you can do so by coating large pieces of extruded foam with sand and grout mixtures. These have the benefit of being much lighter than real rocks, which makes maintenance easier. It also improves the safety of the habitat, as the foam rocks are less likely to injure your lizard, should they fall over. Additionally, you can build rocks that fit your cage precisely, rather than having to adapt your design to suit the rocks you have.

Most of the dwarf monitors inhabit rock outcrops or areas bordering outcrops, and they will utilize such structures in their habitats.

Hiding Spots

All but the largest monitors are spend much of their time hiding. They use a variety of locations for hiding, including rock crevices, abandoned animal burrows and tree hollows. Some monitors even dig their own burrows.

It is vital to your pet's health and well-being to provide them with plenty of suitable hiding spots. These can take a variety of forms, but they all have a few common characteristics:

- Hiding spots must be snug
- Hiding spots must be accessible for the keeper
- Hiding spots must be easy to clean, or cheap enough to replace
- Hiding spots should be dark inside

A few popular choices include cardboard boxes, plastic containers (inverted and fitted with an entrance hole), cork bark, and commercial hiding spots. Additionally, some keepers utilize natural objects, such as hollow logs, or build completely functional, yet artificial hiding places.

Large sections of cork bark are among the best hiding spots for most terrestrial species. They provide snug accommodations, and yet are very light. Cork bark tubes are also very effective, and make excellent hiding and climbing structures for arboreal species. Be careful to avoid the popular – but useless – "half log" style hides, as they are much too tall to provide suitable hiding spots. You can arrange or stack rocks to make hiding places, but you must be careful to stack them so that they cannot fall and injure your lizard. In most cases, you should cement the rocks in place to avoid such accidents.

An excellent way to provide hiding locations for your monitor is by making a stack of spaced wood planks.

Chapter 10: Maintaining the Captive Habitat

Now that you have your lizard and the habitat, you must develop a protocol for maintaining the habitat. You will find that monitors require minor maintenance on a daily maintenance, while they require major maintenance on a monthly basis.

Cleaning Procedures
Once you have decided on the proper cage for your pet, you must keep your lizard fed, hydrated and ensure that the habitat stays in proper working order. This will require you to examine the cage daily to ensure that your lizard is healthy and comfortable.

Some tasks must be completed each day, while others are should be performed weekly, monthly or annually.

Daily
- Monitor the ambient and surface temperatures of the habitat.
- Ensure that the monitor's water bowl is full of clean water.
- Ensure that the lizard has not defecated or produced urates in the cage. If he has, you must clean the cage.
- Ensure that the lights, latches and other moving parts are in working order.
- Verify that your lizard is acting normally and appears healthy. You do not necessarily need to handle him to do so.
- Ensure that the humidity and ventilation are at appropriate levels.

Weekly
- Empty, wash and refill the water container.
- Change any sheet-like substrate.
- Clean the walls of the enclosure.
- Remove your lizard and inspect him for any injuries, parasites or signs of illness.

Monthly
- Break down the cage completely, remove and discard the upper level of substrate.
- Clean the entire cage from top to bottom.
- Sterilize the water dish and any other plastic or ceramic furniture in a mild bleach solution.
- Measure and weigh your lizard.
- Soak your monitor lizard for about 1 hour (Recommended, but not imperative).
- Photograph your pet (Recommended, but not imperative).

Annually
- Visit the veterinarian to ensure that your monitor is in good health.
- Replace the batteries in your thermometers and any other devices that use them.

Cleaning your lizard's cage and furniture is relatively simple. Regardless of the way it became soiled or its constituent materials, the basic process is the same:

1. Rinse the object
2. Using a scrub brush or sponge and soapy water, remove any organic debris from the object.
3. Rinse the object thoroughly.
4. Disinfect the object.
5. Re-rinse the object.
6. Dry the object.

Chemicals & Tools

A variety of chemicals and tools are necessary for reptile care. Save yourself some time by purchasing dedicated cleaning products and keeping them in the same place that you keep your tools.

Scrub Brushes or Sponges

It helps to have a few different types of scrub brushes, sponges and similar tools. Use the least abrasive sponge or brush suitable for the task to prevent wearing out cage items prematurely. Do not use abrasive materials on glass or acrylic surfaces. Steel-bristled brushes work well for scrubbing wooden items, such as branches.

Spatulas and Putty Knives
Spatulas, putty knives and similar tools are often helpful for cleaning reptile cages. For example, urates often become stuck on cage walls or furniture. The best way to remove them is by scraping them with a sturdy plastic putty knife.

Small Vacuums
Small, handheld vacuums are very helpful for sucking up the dust left behind from substrates. They are also helpful for cleaning the tracks that hold sliding glass cage doors. A shop vacuum, with suitable hoses and attachments, can also be helpful.

Steam Cleaners
Steam cleaners are very effective for sterilizing cages, water bowls and durable cage props after they have been cleaned. Steam is a very effective for sterilizing surfaces, and it will not leave behind a toxic residue. Never use a steam cleaner near your lizard or any other living creatures.

Soap
Use gentle, non-scented dish soap. Antibacterial soap is preferred, but not necessary. Most people use far more soap than is necessary -- a few drops mixed with a quantity of water is usually sufficient to help remove surface pollutants.

Bleach
Bleach (diluted to one-half cup per gallon of water) makes an excellent disinfectant. Be careful not to spill any on clothing, carpets or furniture, as it is likely to discolor the objects. Soak water bowls in this type of dilute bleach solution monthly.

Always be sure to rinse objects thoroughly after using bleach and be sure that you cannot detect any residual odor. Bleach does not work as a disinfectant when in contact with organic substances; accordingly, the cage must be cleaned before you can disinfect it.

Veterinarian Approved Disinfectant
Many commercial products are available that are designed to be safe for their pets. Consult with your veterinarian about the best product for your situation, its method of use and its proper dilution.

Avoid Phenols
Always avoid cleaners that contain phenols, as they are extremely toxic to some reptiles. In general, do not use household cleaning products to avoid exposing your pet to toxic chemicals.

Keeping Records
It is important to keep records regarding your pet's health, feeding and other important details. In the past, reptile keepers would do so on small index cards or in a notebook. In the modern world, technological solutions may be easier, such as using your computer or mobile device to keep track of the pertinent info about your pet.

There is no limit to the amount of information you can record about your pet – and the more information to you record, the better. At a minimum, you should record the following:

Pedigree and Origin Information
Be sure to record the source of your lizard, the date on which you acquired him and any other data that is available. If you purchase the monitor from a quality breeder, you will likely be provided with information regarding the sire, dam, date of birth, weights and feeding records.

Feeding Information
At a minimum, record the date and type of food item your lizard eats at each feeding. It is also helpful to record refused meals as well.

If you always feed your spiny-tailed monitor crickets on Mondays, Wednesdays and Fridays, you do not have to write this down. Instead, simply note any time you cannot feed him on this schedule. Likewise, if you feed your adult water two large rats every Saturday and Wednesday, you probably do not need to write it down every time.

Weights and Length
At a minimum, you should record the weight of your lizard monthly. Because you look at your pet frequently, it is difficult to determine his growth rate visually. It is important to track his weight to ensure he is growing properly.

Weigh small monitor lizards using a high quality digital scale. The scale must be sensitive to 1-gram increments to be useful for small lizards. You will need a small plastic container to weigh your lizard.

First, weigh the container (including the lid) and write the weight on the bottom or side for future reference. Then, add the lizard to the container, close the lid, and weigh the container again. Subtract the weight of the container from the combined weight to determine your lizard's mass.

Large lizards can be challenging to weigh. The best way for most keepers to determine the mass of a large lizard is to hold your lizard in your hands and step on a bathroom scale. Subtract your weight from the combined weight of you and your lizard, to find his weight.

If you like, you can measure your monitor lizard's length as well, but doing so is very difficult to produce accurate results. There are computer programs that will calculate the length of your lizard if you photograph him near a ruler.

Maintenance Information
Record the dates and details of any major maintenance. For example, while it is not necessary to note that you topped off the water dish each day, it is appropriate to record the dates on which you changed the substrate, or sterilized the cage.

Whenever you purchase new equipment, supplies or caging, note the date and source. This not only helps to remind you when you purchased the items, but it may help you track down a source for the items in the future, if necessary.

Breeding Information
If you intend on breeding your lizard, you should record all details regarding the pre-breeding conditioning, cycling, introductions, copulations, ovulation, post-ovulation shed and egg deposition. Record all pertinent information about the clutch as well, including the number of viable eggs, as well as the number of unhatched and unfertilized eggs (often called "slugs" by reptile keepers).

Record Keeping Samples
The following are two different examples of suitable recording systems. The first example is reminiscent of the style of card that many breeders and experienced hobbyists use. Because such keepers often have numerous animals, the notes are very simple, and require a minimum amount of writing or typing. Note that in this example, the keeper has employed a simple code, so that he or she does not have to write out "fed this lizard one small, thawed mouse."

ID Number:	44522	Genus: Species/Sub:	Varanus acanthurus	Gender: DOB:	Male 3/20/14	CARD #2
6.30.14 Crickets	7.03.13 Crickets, Superworms	7.08.13 Ground Turkey	7.14.13 Crickets	7.17.13 Crickets		
7.01.14 Crickets	7.05.13 Crickets	7.09.13 Roaches	7.15.13 Superworms, Roaches	7.19.13 Ground Turkey		
7.02.13 Roaches	7.06.13 Crickets	7.12.13 Ground Turkey	7.16.13 Crickets			

The second example demonstrates a simple approach that is employed by many novice keepers – keeping notes on paper. Such notes could be taken in a notebook or journal, or simply typed into a word processor. It does not ultimately matter *how* you keep records, just that you *do* keep records.

Date	Notes
6-22-13	*Acquired ""Godzilla" the savannah monitor from a lizard breeder named Mark at the in-town reptile expo. Mark explained that Godzilla's scientific name is Varanus exanthematicus. Cost was $75. Mark was not sure what sex Monty was, and wasn't sure how to tell. Mark said he purchased the lizard in March, but he does not know the exact date.*
6-23-13	*I have decided to consider Godzilla a boy until he gets big enough to know for sure. He spent the night in the container I bought him in. I purchased a 20-gallon aquarium, screened lid, bag of substrate and heat lamp at the pet store. Bought the thermometer at the hardware store next door and ordered a non-contact thermometer online. I am using old food containers for his water dish. I added a stack of small boards under the basking spot.*
6-27-13	*Godzilla hissed a little when I misted him. He ate a ton of crickets! At least 30.*
6-30-13	*I fed Godzilla a thawed hopper mouse today. I think I need longer tweezers! He was hungry!*
7-1-13	*Since Godzilla looked so hungry, I fed him another thawed mouse today.*
7-3-13	*Fed Godzilla three dozen crickets and a moth that flew into the house. He ate everything and looked like he wanted more.*

Common Husbandry Problems and Solutions

Problem	Solution
Cage too cool	• Increase power / wattage of heating devices • Add additional heating devices • Place heating devices closer to the cage • Incorporate more thermal mass in the cage • Insulate the cage • Reduce the ventilation slightly • Move the cage to a different location
Cage too warm	• Reduce power / wattage of heating devices • Remove some of the heating devices • Use a rheostat / thermostat to reduce temperature • Remove thermal mass from the cage • Move cage to a different location
Cage too dry	• Mist the cage more frequently / thoroughly • Increase the size of the water dish • Use moisture-retaining substrate • Reduce ventilation slightly • Add live plants to the enclosure • Use bubbler in water dish
Cage too damp	• Increase ventilation • Swap live plants for artificial plants • Reduce the size of the water dish • Allow substrate to dry before adding to the cage

Problem	Solution
Retained Sheds	- Increase cage humidity - Include a humid hiding space - Implement a soaking regimen - Ensure the lizard has no health problems (mites, etc.)
Monitor won't eat	- Ensure that the cage has appropriate temperatures. - Experiment with different food items (mice, chicks, rats) - Ensure the lizard is healthy – most monitors have ravenous appetites - Reduce the lizard's stress -- less handling, more privacy
The cage smells	- Clean the cage more often / thoroughly - Switch to paper substrate - Increase cage ventilation
Continuous pacing (beyond normal levels of foraging)	- Ensure cage temperatures are not too high - Ensure your monitor has water - Ensure your monitor is adequately fed - Mature males may be searching for female
Monitor is aggressive	- Ensure the cage is not subject to vibration, etc. - Ensure the cage features enough hiding opportunities - Ensure temperatures are correct - Reduce handling frequency

Chapter 11: Feeding Monitor Lizards

Monitor lizards are obligate carnivores that consume a wide variety of prey in the wild.

Insects
Insects should form the bulk of the diet for most small monitor lizards. Crickets or roaches make a nice staple, while the other insects can be incorporated to add variety.

Most experienced keepers avoid feeding wild caught insects to their monitors, as the insects may be contaminated with pesticides or infested with parasites.

The following insects make suitable prey for monitor lizards:

- Crickets
- Roaches
- Mealworms
- Giant Mealworms
- Superworms
- Wax Worms
- Grasshoppers

Fish
Some semi-aquatic monitors consume fish as part of their natural diet, and most will likely consume fish if offered. Do not offer your monitor goldfish or other "starter" fish, as these are likely to be heavily parasitized.

Rodents
Rodents make up the bulk of the diet for most large species, and a helpful component in the diet of smaller species. However, care must be taken to avoid causing your lizard to become obese, given the high caloric value of mice and rats.

Rodents are available commercially in a range of sizes, from hairless, newborn "pinkies,' to fully-grown, retired breeders.

Birds
Chicks, quail and ducks are often available commercially, and they make excellent food sources for larger monitors. Birds often cause monitors to produce soft, foul-smelling feces. Additionally, feeding a bird-based diet likely increases the chances that your lizard will contract salmonella.

Eggs
Eggs are an excellent occasional supplementary food item for your lizards. You can simply give them to your lizard as is, or you can boil them until the yolk sets, which will reduce the bacterial load present in the egg. Eggs make up a significant portion of the diet of some species, and it is one of the few "human" foods that are suitable for monitors. Your monitor may eat the whole egg if he is big enough, or he may break it and lap out the contents.

Smaller lizards can be offered full sized eggs, but you can also find quail eggs at some grocery stores. These small eggs are an excellent option for mature dwarf monitors.

This lace monitor is eating an egg. Most monitor lizards relish eggs, and they form an important part of the diet of many species.

Live, Fresh Killed or Frozen
Monitor lizards are completely capable of dispatching suitably sized prey, but it is best to offer frozen-thawed or pre-killed rodents and birds to your pet. Not only is it possible that a rodent

or bird may injure your lizard, being stalked, captured and eaten by a hungry lizard is very stressful (to say the least) for the mouse, rat or bird. It is preferable to euthanize prey animals humanely or purchase those that are frozen.

Freezing also kills some pathogens, so frozen-thawed rodents are likely healthier for your monitor.

Prey Size

Monitor lizards can eat large meals, but there is no need to provide food at the upper end of their range. In general, food items should be smaller than the space between the lizard's eyes.

This is especially important for young animals, whose heads are very large relative to their body size. Monitor lizards can experience problems from swallowing prey that is too big, and it often causes them to vomit.

How to Offer Food

You can simply release crickets and other insects into your monitor's cage. This will also provide exercise for your monitor and mental stimulation. However, it is often better to place burrowing insects – mealworms, roaches, etc. – on a feeding dish so that they do not tunnel out of sight.

Some keepers like to place a group of mealworms on a plate, and then cover them with a big pile of dirt or mulch. The lizard will usually smell the insects, and get exercise by digging them out of the dirt or mulch.

Offer your monitor frozen rodents or birds by dangling these items in front of their face with long tongs or tweezers. Monitors get very excited at feeding time, so you must be careful to avoid their sharp teeth.

Do not allow large numbers of feeder insects to roam the enclosure freely, as it can stress your monitor. Additionally, the crickets may feed on your monitor's delicate skin near his eyes and vent.

This does not mean that you cannot offer a large lizard a significant number of insects at one time. It just means that you should only give your monitor as many insects as he can eat in a short period of time. Once he is full, the cage should be free of insects.

Frozen-thawed rodents are an excellent food source for monitor lizards.

Feeding Frequency

The proper feeding frequency for your monitor depends on his size, species and age. Generally speaking, monitor lizards should be fed three to six times per week; the younger the lizard, the more often it should be fed.

As long as your monitor is healthy, gets plenty of exercise, has access to suitable temperatures and is provided with a wide variety of food items, you do not have to worry about overfeeding him. However, mature monitors – or those living in small cages – may become overweight if fed too frequently.

Ultimately, you must adjust your lizard's diet by monitoring his weight regularly. Young lizards should exhibit steady, moderate growth rates, while mature animals should maintain a relatively consistent body weight.

If your lizard begins losing weight, you must increase the frequency of his feedings. Conversely, those that gain excessive wait should be placed on restrictive diets. Consult with your veterinarian before altering your feeding schedule drastically.

The charts below detail a few examples of suitable diets:

Hatchling spiny-tailed monitor

Monday	Crickets
Tuesday	Crickets
Wednesday	Silkworms
Thursday	*Nothing*
Friday	Crickets
Saturday	Crickets
Sunday	Roaches

Juvenile yellow-spotted monitor

Monday	Crickets
Tuesday	2 mice
Wednesday	Superworms
Thursday	*Nothing*
Friday	Crickets
Saturday	2 mice
Sunday	Roaches

Adult white-throated monitor

Monday	2 Rats
Tuesday	4 Eggs
Wednesday	*Nothing*
Thursday	Roaches
Friday	2 Rats
Saturday	4 Eggs
Sunday	*Nothing*

You can divide a day's food into two or three servings, offered throughout the day if you wish. This will allow your lizard to ingest more food throughout the course of the day, as the earlier meals work their way down the lizard's digestive system.

Safety at Feeding Time

Well-conditioned monitor lizards often rush to the front of the cage – mouth open – at feeding time. This can lead to serious accidents, so it is important to act with care.

Rather than opening the cage, then grabbing the food item, then finding your tongs, is completely prepared before opening the cage. Always be sure that the room is calm before opening the cage, and that no children or other pets are present.

Chapter 12: Hydrating Your Monitor Lizard

Like most other animals, monitor lizards require drinking water to remain healthy. However, the amount of water in the air (humidity) is an important factor in their health as well.

Drinking Water

Providing drinking water is as simple as adding a small water dish to the cage. Monitors can smell water, and, unlike some other species, they will drink readily from a dish.

For those species that swim regularly, it is advisable to provide a water dish that is large enough to contain the entire lizard. However, because monitor lizards often defecate in the water, you must clean the water dish frequently to prevent them from drinking fouled water.

Although many monitor lizards hailing from arid habitats appear to get most of their water from their food, keepers should provide captives with drinking water at all times.

Some keepers like to give their monitors dechlorinated or purified, bottled water, but this is not necessary. Plenty of monitors have been raised in captivity while drinking ordinary tap water.

Humidity

Most keepers will achieve suitable humidity levels by simply incorporating a large water dish into the habitat. The volume of water is not as important as the surface area of the water. In other words, a shallow, wide dish will raise the cage humidity more than a narrow, deeper water bowl will.

Placing the water dish under a heat lamp or over a heating pad will help accelerate the evaporation rate, but it will require you to refill the water dish more frequently.

You can also dampen the substrate to elevate the humidity level inside the cage. The damp (not wet) substrate will slowly release the water into the air in the cage, thus elevating the humidity. This works best with moisture-retaining substrates, such as cypress mulch or orchid bark. However, you can also dampen newspaper and similar substrates.

Misting
Another way to raise the humidity in the cage is by misting the substrate and interior surfaces of the enclosure with lukewarm water.

It is perfectly safe to spray your lizard (gently) with clean, lukewarm water, but be aware that some individuals do not like to be sprayed. Your lizard may begin drinking or simply flee.

Keepers with one small monitor lizard will usually find a simple, handheld spray bottle to be sufficient. Keepers with many reptiles or a very large specimen are better served by acquiring a compressed-air sprayer.

Always allow the standing water droplets to evaporate or soak into the substrate between mistings – the cage should not stay wet for extended periods of time.

In addition to increasing the cage humidity temporarily, misting often causes monitor lizards to become active. This benefits them by encouraging exercise, mental stimulation, and, often, it causes them to defecate. Misting is also a stimulus used to elicit mating behavior.

One drawback to misting cages is that the water droplets can leave unsightly spots on glass surfaces. Water with a low-mineral content may help eliminate this possibility.

Restricting Airflow
Cages with excess ventilation, such as many aquaria, may allow too much water to evaporate from the cage. To prevent this from happening, you can attach a piece of glass or plastic to a portion of the screened areas of the cage. This will reduce the amount of water that evaporates from the cage. You do not want to reduce the ventilation too much, so only cover as much of the cage as is necessary to raise the humidity.

If you use an air conditioner in your home during the summer or the heater during the winter, you may find that your cages dry out faster than normal. Both such units reduce the humidity of the air in your home, which will tend to draw moisture out of the cage.

Soaking Your Lizard

In addition to providing drinking water, many keepers soak their monitor lizards periodically in a tub of clean, lukewarm water. Soaking is helpful tool for the husbandry of many reptiles, especially those who hail from very humid habitats.

In addition to ensuring that your pet remains adequately hydrated, soaks help to remove dirt and encourage complete, problem-free sheds. It is not necessary to soak your lizard if it remains adequately hydrated, but most benefit from an occasional soak.

Soaks should last a maximum of about one hour, and be performed no more often than once per week (unless the lizard is experiencing shedding difficulties).

When soaking your pet, the water should not be very deep. Never make your lizard swim to keep its head above water. Ideally, monitor lizards should be soaked in containers with only enough water to cover their back. This should allow them to rest comfortably with its head above water.

Never leave your pet unattended while it is soaking.

If the monitor defecates in the water, be sure to rinse him off with clean water before returning him to his cage.

Chapter 13: Interacting with Monitor Lizards
Handling

The best way to hold a small monitor lizard is by placing it in the palm of your hand, and pressing lightly on its back with your thumb. Defensive monitors can still bite when held like this, but their bites are usually inconsequential.

Larger monitors are best held by laying them across your arm, with your hand under their throat. Spread your fingers so that the legs can dangle between them. Place the tail between your upper arm and rib cage to keep it from flapping around.

Very large monitors are difficult to hold. It usually takes two people to restrain a large lizard adequately, but if your lizard is tame, you may be able to handle him normally.

In The Event of a Bite

In the unfortunate event of a bite, your first task is to immobilize the lizard to prevent him from thrashing with his head. The teeth of a monitor will cause puncture wounds, and the pressure of the bite may hurt, but these problems will become exacerbated if the lizard moves his head. This will turn the puncture wounds into deep lacerations.

After immobilizing your lizard's head, you can try to slide something smooth and flat into the monitor's mouth. This may help you extricate the teeth from one jaw from your flesh. If this does not cause the lizard to release his grip voluntarily, do the same thing with his bottom jaw.

Once you have a barrier on each jaw, you can simply remove your hand, finger or arm.

If you cannot get the lizard to release his grip, you can plunge him in a bucket of cold water. Unfortunately, many monitors can hold their breath for 30 minutes or more, so you may be in for a long wait.

Temporary Transport Cages
The best way to transport your lizard is with a plastic storage container. The container must have ample air holes to allow ventilation and it must be safe and secure.

Some keepers prefer transparent boxes for such purposes, as they allow you to see the animal while it is inside the box. This is definitely a benefit – especially when opening and closing the box – but opaque transportation boxes provide your pet with more security, as they cannot see the activity going on outside their container.

Place a few paper towels or some clean newspaper in the bottom of the box to give your lizard somewhere to hide and to absorb any fluids, should your lizard defecate or discharge urates.

Transporting Tips
When traveling with your monitor lizard, pay special attention to the temperature. Use the air-conditioning or heater in your vehicle to keep the animal within his comfortable range (the mid-70s Fahrenheit are ideal in most circumstances).

Do not jostle your pet unnecessarily, nor leave it unattended in a car. Make sure that the transport container is secure – in the unfortunate circumstance in which you are in an accident, a loose monitor lizard is not an additional problem with which you need to contend.

Do not take your lizard with you on public transportation.

Hygiene
Always practice good hygiene when handling reptiles. Wash your hands with soap and warm water each time you touch your pet, his habitat or the tools you use to care for him.

Never wash cages or tools in kitchens or bathrooms that are used by humans.

Chapter 14: Common Health Concerns

Unlike humans, who can tell you when they are sick, reptiles endure illness stoically. This does not mean that injury or illnesses do not cause them distress, but without expressive facial features, they do not look like they are suffering.

In fact, many reptile illnesses do not produce symptoms until the disease has already reached an advanced state. Accordingly, it is important to treat injuries and illness promptly to provide your pet with the best chance of recovery.

Acquiring competent veterinary care for a monitor lizard is not as easy as finding a veterinarian to treat a dog or cat. Those living in major metropolitan areas are likely to find one reasonably close, but rural reptile keepers may have to take great lengths to find a suitable vet.

Finding a Suitable Veterinarian
Relatively few veterinarians treat reptiles. It is important to find a reptile-oriented veterinarian before you need one. There are a number of ways to do this:

- You can search veterinarian databases to find one that is local and treats reptiles.
- You can inquire with your dog or cat veterinarian to see if he or she knows a qualified reptile-oriented veterinarian to whom he or she can refer you.
- You can contact a local reptile-enthusiast group or club. Most such organizations will be familiar with the local veterinarians.
- You can inquire with local nature preserves or zoos. Most such institutions have relationships with veterinarians that treat reptiles and other exotic animals.

If you happen to live in a remote area and do not have a reptile-oriented veterinarian within driving distance, you can try to find a conventional veterinarian who will treat your animal after consulting with a reptile-oriented veterinarian. Such visits may be expensive, as you will have to pay for two veterinary visits (the actual visit and the phone consultation), but it may be your only choice.

Reasons to Visit the Veterinarian

While reptiles do not require vaccinations or similar routine treatments, they may require visits for other reasons. Anytime your lizard exhibits signs of illness or suffers an injury, you must visit the veterinarian.

Visit your veterinarian when:

- You first acquire your pet. This will allow your veterinarian to familiarize himself or herself with the animal while it is presumably healthy. This gives him or her a baseline against which he or she can consider future deviations. Additionally, your veterinarian may be able to diagnose existing illnesses, before they cause serious problems.
- Anytime your lizard wheezes, exhibits labored breathing or produces a mucus discharge from its nostrils or mouth.
- Your monitor produces soft or watery feces. (Soft feces are expected when lizards are fed some food items, such as birds. This is not necessarily cause for concern.)
- Your reptile suffers any significant injury. Common examples include thermal burns, friction damage to the rostral (nose) region or damaged scales.
- Reproductive issues occur, such as being unable to deliver young. If a lizard appears nervous, agitated or otherwise stressed and unable to expel eggs, see your veterinarian immediately.
- Your lizard fails to feed for an extended period.

Common Health Problems

Some of the common health problems, their causes and suggested course of action follow.

Retained or Poor Sheds

Most monitor lizards shed over an extended period of time, which often causes them to retain large portions of their old skin. This is not usually a big problem, but care must be taken to ensure that the face, tail tip and toes all shed completely to avoid health problems. Retained skin in these places can restrict blood flow, and cause the loss of the tail tip or toes.

Nevertheless, monitor lizards look their best when they have just shed their skin completely. With a little effort on your part, you can help your lizard to look his best.

The best way to remove retained sheds is by soaking your lizard or placing him in a damp container for about an hour. After removing him, see if you can gently peel the skin off. Try to keep the skin in as few pieces as possible to make the job easier.

Do not force the skin off your lizard. If it does not come off easily, return him to his cage and repeat the process again in 12 to 24 hours. Usually, repeated soaks or time in a damp hide will loosen the skin sufficiently to be removed.

If repeated treatments do not yield results, consult your veterinarian. He may feel that the retained shed is not causing a problem, and advise you to leave it attached – it should come off with the next shed. Alternatively, it if is causing a problem, the veterinarian can remove it without much risk of harming your pet.

Respiratory Infections

Like humans, lizards can suffer from respiratory infections. Monitor lizards with respiratory infections exhibit fluid or mucus draining from their nose and/or mouth, may be lethargic and are unlikely to eat. They may also spend excessive amounts of time basking on or under the heat source, in an effort to induce a "behavioral fever."

Bacteria, or, less frequently, fungi or parasites often cause respiratory infections. In addition, cleaning products, perfumes, pet dander and other particulate matter can irritate a reptile's respiratory tract as well. Some such bacteria are ubiquitous, and only become problematic when they overwhelm an animal's immune system. Other bacteria (and most viruses) are transmitted from one lizard to another.

To reduce the chances of illnesses, keep your lizard separated from other lizards, keep his enclosure exceptionally clean and be sure to provide the best husbandry possible, in terms of temperature and humidity. Additionally, avoid stressing your pet by handling him too frequently, or exposing him to chaotic situations.

Upon taking your pet to the vet, he or she will likely take samples of the mucus and have it analyzed to determine the causal agent. The veterinarian will then prescribe medications, if appropriate, such as antibiotics.

It is imperative to carry out the actions prescribed by your veterinarian exactly as stated, and keep your lizard's stress level very low while he is healing. Stress can reduce immune function, so avoid handling him unnecessarily, and consider covering the front of his cage while he recovers.

"Mouth Rot"
Mouth rot – properly called stomatitis – is identified by noting discoloration, discharge or cheesy-looking material in your monitor's mouth. Mouth rot can be a serious illness, and requires the attention of your veterinarian.

While mouth rot can follow an injury (such as happens when a lizard rubs his snout against the sides of the cage) it can also arise from systemic illness. Your veterinarian will cleanse your lizard's mouth and potentially prescribe an antibiotic.

Your veterinarian may recommend withholding food until the problem is remedied. Always be sure that lizards recovering from mouth rot have immaculately clean habitats, with ideal temperatures.

Internal Parasites
In the wild, most monitor lizards carry some internal parasites. While it may not be possible to keep a reptile completely free of internal parasites, it is important to keep these levels in check.

Consider any wild-caught animals to be parasitized until proven otherwise. While most captive bred monitors should have relatively few internal parasites, they can suffer from such problems as well.

Preventing parasites from building to pathogenic levels requires strict hygiene. Many parasites build up to dangerous levels when lizards are kept in cages that are continuously contaminated from feces.

Most internal parasites that are of importance for lizards are transmitted via the fecal-oral route. This means that eggs (or a similar life stage) of the parasites are released with the feces. If the monitor inadvertently ingests these, the parasites can develop inside his body and cause increased problems. Such eggs are usually microscopic and easily lifted into the air, where they may stick to cage walls or land in the water dish. Later, when the monitor flicks its tongue or drinks from the water dish, it ingests the eggs.

Internal parasites may cause your lizard to vomit, pass loose stools, and fail to grow or refuse food entirely. Other parasites may produce no symptoms at all, demonstrating the importance of routine examinations.

Your veterinarian will usually examine your pet's feces if he suspects internal parasites. By looking at the type of eggs inside the feces, your veterinarian can prescribe an appropriate medication. Many parasites are easily treated with anti-parasitic medications, but often, these medications must be given several times to eradicate the pathogens completely.

Some parasites may be transmissible to people, so always take proper precautions, including regular hand washing and keeping reptiles and their cages away from kitchens and other areas where foods are prepared.

Examples of common internal parasites include roundworms, tapeworms and amoebas.

External Parasites

The primary external parasites that afflict monitor lizards are ticks and mites. Ticks are rare on captive bred animals, but wild caught monitors often have a few.

Ticks should be removed manually. Using tweezers grasp the tick as close as possible to the lizard's skin and pull with steady, gentle pressure. Do not place anything over the tick first, such as petroleum jelly, or carry out any other "home remedies," such as burning the tick with a match. Such techniques may cause the tick to inject more saliva (which may contain diseases or bacteria) into the monitor's body.

Drop the tick in a jar of isopropyl alcohol to ensure it is killed. It is a good idea to bring these to your veterinarian for analysis. Do not contact ticks with your bare hands, as many species can transmit disease to humans.

Mites are another matter entirely. While ticks are generally large enough to see easily, mites are about the size of a pepper flake. Whereas tick infestations usually only tally a few individuals, mite infestations may include thousands of individual parasites.

Mites may afflict wild caught lizards, but, as they are not confined to a small cage, such infestations are somewhat self-limiting. However, in captivity, mite infestations can approach plague proportions.

After a female mite feeds on a lizard, she drops off and finds a safe place (such as a tiny crack in a cage or among the substrate) to deposit her eggs. After the eggs hatch, they travel back to your pet (or to other lizards in your collection) where they feed and perpetuate the lifecycle.

Whereas a few mites may represent little more than an inconvenience to the lizard, a significant infection stresses them considerably, and may even cause death through anemia. This is particularly true for small or young animals. Additionally, mites may transmit disease from one animal to another.

There are a number of different methods for eradicating a mite infestation. In each case, there are two primary steps that must be taken: You must eradicate the lizard's parasites, and eradicate the parasites in the environment (which includes the room in which the cage resides).

It is relatively simple to remove mites from a lizard. When mites get wet, they die. However, mites are protected by a thick, waxy exoskeleton that encourages the formation of an air bubble. This means that you cannot place your monitor in water to drown the mites. The mites will simply hide under the lizard's scales, using their air bubble to protect themselves.

To defeat this waxy cuticle, all that is needed is a few drops of gentle dish soap added to the water. The soap will lower the surface tension of water, allowing it to penetrate under the lizard's scales. Additionally, the soap disrupts the surface tension of the water, preventing the air bubble from forming.

Soaking your monitor is the slightly soapy water for about one hour will kill most of the mites on his body. Use care when doing so, but try to arrange the water level and container so that most of his body is below the water.

While the monitor is soaking, perform a thorough cage cleaning. Remove everything from the cage, including water dishes, substrates and cage props. Sterilize all impermeable cage items, and discard the substrate and all porous cage props. Vacuum the area around the cage and wipe down all of the nearby surfaces with a wet cloth.

It may be necessary to repeat this process several times to eradicate the mites completely. Accordingly, the very best strategy is to avoid contracting mites in the first place. This is why it is important to purchase your monitor lizard from a reliable breeder or retailer, and keep him quarantined from potential mite vectors.

As an example, even if you purchase your lizard from a reliable source, provide excellent husbandry and clean the cage regularly, you can end up battling mites if your friend brings his lizard – which has a few mites – to your house.

It may be possible for mites to crawl onto your hands or clothes, hop off when you return home and make their way to your monitor. This is why many breeders and experienced hobbyists avoid visiting low-quality pet stores or places with poorly tended cages.

While it is relatively easy to observe mites on a lizard that has a significant infestation, a few mites may go unnoticed. Make it a practice to inspect your pet and his cage regularly. Look in the crease under his lower jaw, near the eyes and near the vent; all of these are places in which mites hide. It can also be helpful to wipe down your monitor with a damp, white paper towel. After wiping down the lizard, observe the towel to see if any mites are present.

Chemical treatments are also available to combat mites, but you must be very careful with such substances. Beginners should rely on their veterinarian to prescribe or suggest the appropriate chemicals.

Avoid repurposing lice treatments or other chemicals, as is often encouraged by other hobbyists. Such non-intended use may be very dangerous, and it is often in violation of Federal laws.

New hobbyists should consult with their veterinarian if they suspect that their lizard has mites. Mite eradication is often a challenging ordeal that your veterinarian can help make easier.

Long-Term Anorexia
While monitor lizards may refuse the occasional meal, they should not fast for prolonged periods of time, unless they are being cycled for breeding (in which case the temperatures may be

lower for some time). Even then, most monitors exhibit healthy appetites.

The most common reasons that monitors refuse food are improper temperatures and illness. Parasites and bacterial infections often cause monitors to refuse food. Consult your veterinarian anytime that your lizard refuses food for longer than five to seven days.

Chapter 15: Breeding Monitor Lizards

Monitor lizards are not bred with the frequency of some other popular reptile pets. This likely precipitates from a combination of factors, including the large size of many species and the lack of information regarding the breeding biology and behavior of most species.

Additionally, relatively few captive bred monitors are available in the first place – as wild caught animals are very difficult to acclimate and breed, it is usually much easier to get captive bred animals to breed successfully. Obviously, this is something of a catch-22, as a small group of breeders must have "breakthrough" success to provide the captive stock, which makes further clutches more likely.

Nevertheless, monitor lizards have been bred with increasing regularity in the last few decades. Many of the dwarf monitors – especially spiny-tailed monitors – are bred with relative regularity. However, large species are rarely offered for sale as true captive bred offspring. Instead, the young animals seen in the pet trade are usually farmed offspring, imported from Asian and African countries. In such farms, the adult lizards are kept in a pseudo-wild manner, and the eggs or young are collected and shipped to markets.

Even for those species that are bred with regularity, few reliable "formulas" for breeding success have been devised. Nevertheless, most keepers embrace a relatively similar approach.

Sexing Monitor Lizards

Obviously, you must have at least one sexual pair to breed monitor lizards. However, it can be difficult to determine the gender of monitor lizards.

The males of some species, such as spiny-tailed monitors, have enlarged scale clusters at both sides of the vent. Others have large, visible hemipenal bulges, which indicate their gender. Some keepers have had success probing their monitor lizards, but this is a difficult task that should only be attempted by experienced keepers or veterinarians. Young monitor lizards may be sexed by manually everting their hemipenes, although this only positively identifies males – those that fail to evert hemipenes may be females or males, who for one reason or another, did not allow their hemipenes to evert.

Males of some species develop telltale secondary sexual characteristics, such as larger size or broader heads. In many cases, these characteristics differ from one species to the next.

If, after examining every criteria possible, you still cannot determine the gender of your lizard, consult with your veterinarian, who may be able to determine your lizard's sex through an endoscopic examination.

It bears mentioning that some keepers and breeders have observed that groups of dwarf monitors that are kept together from a young age rarely develop into single-gender groups. In other words, it appears that some of the lizards may change sex, or have their sex established in response to social cues.

Nevertheless, there is no evidence that this is the case, and all monitors studied to date exhibit genetically determined sex determination. (D, 1975)

Pre-Breeding Conditioning

Before attempting to breed your monitors, you must be sure your lizards are in perfect health. They should have excellent body weight, but not be obese; and they should be free of parasites, infections and injuries.

Breeding is a stressful event for monitors – particularly for the females who must withstand potential injuries during mating, and produce numerous, nutrient-rich eggs. Because of this, it is always best to avoid breeding animals that are not in excellent health.

Some breeders keep their animals together as a matter of course, while others maintain individuals separately and only introduce them for breeding attempts. Both strategies have proven effective in different situations, with different animals. As a general rule, dwarf monitors are often kept together throughout the year. In the wild, some species form relatively high-density populations in small areas, and so they have likely evolved behaviors and tolerances that allow them to coexist peacefully.

Other monitors are prone to fighting with conspecifics. This is especially true of large species, when they are kept in small cages. In these cases, breeders often attempt to keep the animals separate for most of the year, and then pair them briefly during breeding attempts.

Cycling

Some monitor lizards – particularly those from seasonal climates – may require varying temperature and photoperiods throughout the year. Others may successfully reproduce under constant conditions. Ultimately, you as a breeder must decide which approach is best for you and your animals.

To cycle your animals, begin gradually reducing the photoperiod until the animals have about 8 hours of light, and 16 hours of darkness. Continue to provide a heat lamp and basking spot; just restrict the number of hours that the basking spot is heated.

This allows your animals to raise their body temperature for a brief time each day, which allows their immune system to function well, even during the "winter."

Some breeders stop feeding the lizards entirely during this period, while others offer very small, infrequent meals. It is important to ensure that your lizards can still digest food adequately while cool.

Do not be surprised if your lizards exhibit reduced or absent appetites and become somewhat withdrawn, during this time. They will likely spend increasing periods of time sleeping in their hiding spots.

The duration of "winter" should be about 45 to 60 days, depending on the home range of the species. Those hailing from areas with long winters should be cycled for longer than those hailing from milder climates should.

When you are ready to return the conditions to normal, gradually increase the photoperiod, until you are again offering 12 to 14 hours of "daylight."

Pairing

Once the lizards have been cycled, begin feeding them heavily. After a week or two, you can begin pairing the animals.

Introducing unfamiliar animals requires caution – in a worst-case scenario, the larger animal (usually the male) may attack and kill the perceived intruder. Whether this is done out of territorial desires or as an act of predation, the result is the same.

If the animals do not get along, they must be separated, although you may be able to try to pair the animals again in the future. Some breeders design cages that feature a slotted, Plexiglas divider. This way, the animals can see and smell each other for an extended period of time before they have physical contact with each other.

If the pair is compatible, they will likely copulate. They may do this in seclusion, or right in the middle of the cage, so the activity is often missed by keepers.

Gravid

With some luck, the female will become gravid (pregnant) shortly after the animals have bred. While there are no definitive indications that the female is definitively gravid, a few clues may indicate that she is holding eggs.

Many times, gravid females bask for prolonged periods of time. Sometimes, their appetite increases markedly once their eggs begin developing. Near the end of the gestation, females often develop very plump abdomens. In some cases, the faint outline of eggs can be seen.

Handle gravid females as little as possible, and try to keep their stress level as low as possible. If you do not keep the male and female together all year, separate them once you are sure the female is gravid.

Egg Deposition
Providing a suitable place for the female to deposit eggs can be challenging. Sometimes, females do not find a suitable place to lay eggs, and decide to do so in the water dish or other inappropriate places in the cage.

If you use a suitable substrate in the cage, the female will likely dig a small burrow and deposit their eggs directly into the dirt. Otherwise, you will need to place a suitable egg-deposition chamber in the cage, such as a plastic container filled with potting soil.

Egg Incubation
To incubate the eggs artificially, you will need some type of incubator. Beginners should purchase an entry-level, commercially produced product, but advanced keepers can construct their own.

Incubators need not be elaborate to produce good results, but they must be well insulated and maintain a very consistent internal temperature. Always use a separate thermometer as a backup to the incubator's thermometer.

Most often, the eggs are placed in small egg boxes, which are in turn placed in the incubator. Virtually any small plastic boxes will suffice for containing the eggs.

Some keepers place moistened vermiculite or perlite in the egg boxes as a substrate. Other keepers suspend the eggs directly over water. Both strategies can generate success, but vermiculite offers more room for error. Moisten the vermiculite just enough so that it clumps when squeezed in the hand.

You can incubate most monitor eggs between 86 and 88 degrees Fahrenheit. The humidity should be as high as possible, without causing condensation to form on or over the eggs. Eggs do require fresh air, but a few very small (1/8th inch) holes suffice.

The incubation duration varies from one species to the next. Many hatch in about 12 to 13 weeks. The young do not all emerge at once and the earliest hatchlings may emerge up to 48 hours or so before the last emerge.

Do not remove hatchlings from their eggs. Doing so may cause their umbilicus to tear, opening them to infection and cutting off a vital energy source. If any emerge and are still connected to the yolk, allow it to fall off on its own.

Neonatal Husbandry

Once the young begin hatching from their eggs, you can remove them from the egg box and place them in a small cage or "nursery." The nursery should provide the young with constantly appropriate temperatures and relatively high humidity. Temperatures should not drop below 80 degrees in the nursery, during the day or night.

Include several more hides than the total number of lizards in the nursery, to ensure that every lizard has a place to hide. Include a small, shallow water dish.

Leave the neonates in the nursery for about one week. At this time, you can move them to their standard habitats.

Most neonates will begin eating within about one week of hatching. Be sure to offer the young lizards suitably small prey to ensure that they do not choke.

Chapter 16: Good Pet Species

The following species can make suitable pets, if you can provide all of their needs.

Suitable Pet Species of the Odatria Complex

Many monitors of the Odatria complex are bred in captivity, and all have broadly similar husbandry requirements. They are often easy to handle, have interesting personalities and are widely available as captive bred offspring.

Spiny-Tailed Goannas

Spiny-tailed goannas, and most of their relatives, are among the best monitor lizards for captivity. Their small size is the primary reason, as most species fail to exceed 2 feet in length. Additionally, most can be raised in communal enclosures without fear of fighting.

The vast majority of spiny-tailed goannas are captive bred, which provides keepers with a better chance for success. While they are not the tamest species, and may be flighty, most are small enough that difficult temperaments can be overcome.

Spiny-tailed goannas need roomy, dry enclosures with very warm basking sites. They need plenty of rock piles and basking spots for hiding and foraging.

If you intend to breed spiny-tailed goannas, you should try to acquire a group of three or four hatchlings. After a brief quarantine period, they should be introduced to the same cage and kept in this group as long as possible.

Freckled and Mournful Goannas

Freckled goannas occur in two subspecies, *Varanus tristis tristis* – the mournful goanna – and Varanus tristis orientalis – the freckled goanna. Mournful goannas have black heads, which give them their common names. Aside from their differences in coloration, the two subspecies thrive under similar husbandry regimens.

Freckled and mournful goannas are both arboreal species, so they require cages with plenty of climbing opportunities. (Pianka, Notes of the Biology of Varanus Tristis, 1971)

Kimberly Rock Goannas
Kimberly rock goannas are one of the largest members of the subgenus Odatria. They are long, thin lizards that inhabit rock outcrops in Western Australia.

Kimberley rock goannas primarily consume lizards in the wild, but they adapt well to an insect-based diet. These fast lizards are often somewhat flighty, and do not appreciate handling, but they make excellent captives in most other respects.

Kimberly rock goannas are among the most attractive monitors, and they are clad in a beautiful combination of circles and bands. These lizards occasionally exhibit blue and orange tones.

Kimberly rock goannas are not as commonly bred as spiny-tailed monitors are, but they are suitable for beginners who can find them.

Suitable Pet Species of the Euprepiosaurus Subgenus
Species of the genus Euprepiosaurus are usually tropical, forest- or mangrove-dwelling monitors that reach moderate sizes. Few are bred with any regularity, so most captives are wild caught animals. New keepers should strive to acquire captive bred animals whenever possible; failing this, new keepers should acquire the youngest animals possible, as these are usually afflicted with fewer parasites and pathogens. Veterinary attention is required to ensure that these lizards adapt well and thrive.

Green Tree Monitors
Green tree monitors – and their close relatives – are potentially suitable for captivity. They grow to about 3 feet (1 meter) in length, so they are not onerous to house, and they have relatively straightforward husbandry requirements. However, because they are somewhat shy, and require elaborate, rainforest style cages, they are not ideal choices for beginners.

Additionally, green tree monitors are not bred in captivity with any regularity, which means that the vast majority of specimens available are wild caught. These lizards are invariably stricken with internal parasites, and may require extended periods to settle into their new homes.

Green tree monitors are primarily insect-eaters. Most of the prey found in the stomach contents of museum specimens consists of large stick insects, katydids and roaches, although some specimens had consumed rodents as well. (Greene, 1986).

Hobbyists who wish to keep green tree monitors should start with a captive bred specimen.

Mangrove Monitors

Mangrove monitors occasionally reach more than 4 feet in length, but most fail to reach this size. Mangrove monitors – and their close relatives, the blue-tailed and peach-throated monitors, are highly aquatic in the wild, so they should be provided with suitably large swimming pools.

Most mangrove monitors adapt well to captivity, although they are often flighty lizards that seldom learn to accept regular handling.

Suitable Pet Species of the Polydaedalus Subgenus

Some of the smaller African monitors are suitable pets. Most species from the subgenus inhabit open habitats, such as savannahs, open forests and areas along rivers. Almost all African monitors have very strong jaw muscles and blunt molars for crushing mollusk shells.

Savannah Monitors

Savannah monitors are one of the most commonly kept monitor species. Savannah monitors can make suitable captives, provided that one starts with a young lizard and has adequate space to devote to their lizard.

Savannah monitors reach about 3 feet in length, so while they are much more manageable than some other species, they require cages with at least 20 to 30 square feet of space, which is more than most keepers are capable of providing.

Savannah monitors often become tame, trusting captives but they are prone to lethargy and obesity if not fed an appropriate diet and kept in sufficiently large cages.

White-throated Monitors

White throated monitors are closely related and similar to savannah monitors. The primary difference between the species that affects keepers is the size of the animals. Whereas savannah monitors grow to about 3 feet in length, white throated monitors may reach 5 feet in length. Additionally, white throated monitors are massive and powerful animals that are difficult for inexperienced keepers to control.

White throated monitors require about 40 to 50 square feet of space to thrive. Because these monitors are skilled climbers, large tree-like structures should be placed in the habitat. Additionally, it is important to provide these monitors with a substrate that allows the animals to burrow.

Suitable Pet Species of the Varanus Subgenus

Most of the members of the Varanus subgenus are relatively large, terrestrial monitors of Australia and/or New Guinea. Most, such as lace and Perentie goannas, are much too big for beginning hobbyists. However, one complex of three closely related species is suitable for keepers with plenty of space for relatively large lizards.

Yellow-Spotted, Sand Goannas and Desert Sand Goannas
These three distinct species are closely related, and – for the purposes of most keepers – similar in terms of behavior, diet and biology.

Historically, members of all three species were lumped together under the *Varanus gouldii* umbrella. Others considered them members of the *panoptes* species, which has since been discarded. Some authorities fail to recognize three distinct forms, or regard them as subspecies of each other.

Because of this confusion, it can be hard to distinguish which comments, research and observations can be attributed to which of the three forms.

Nevertheless, all three require warm, desert-style cages with plenty of deep substrate that will hold a burrow. These monitors employ badger-like foraging strategies, and they secure most of their food by digging it up or foraging.

These monitors reach up to about 4 feet in length, but because of their activity level, they require very large cages with at least 30 square feet of space.

All three of these monitor species may stand in a tripodal stance, balancing on their rear legs and tail, to survey their surroundings and intimidate adversaries. While they do not climb very often, a tall cage will allow this behavior to take place.

Chapter 17: Generally Inappropriate Pet Species

Many of the living monitors make poor pets. They are generally too large, aggressive or dangerous for amateurs to care for. Unfortunately, many of these species are commonly offered for sale.

When these species wind up in the hands of inexperienced, unprepared keepers, both parties suffer. Ultimately, the lizard ends up receiving substandard care, causing them to languish. If the owner is lucky enough to avoid being injured by their pet, they will surely regret the decision to purchase it, as the cost, labor and difficult involved in caring for the animal are significant.

While experienced keepers and professionals may be able to keep the following species, beginners should absolutely avoid the following species.

Nile Monitors

Nile monitor hatchlings are very handsome, black and gold lizards. They are often tame, eat readily and are offered for sale via many retail avenues – often for a very low price.

Unfortunately, within a few months' time, the small, attractive, tame pet turns into a 3-foot-long beast, that does not allow interaction with their keepers. If you try to hold the lizard, he is likely to run, slap with his tail, hiss, bite and scratch.

These defensive behaviors are daunting enough when the lizard is still relatively small, but once he reaches 5 or 6 feet in length, he becomes positively dangerous. Many animal control officers have remarked that – pound for pound -- Nile monitors are more dangerous than dogs, crocodilians and tigers.

A very few specimens occasionally become tame, but their ultimate size and potential for aggressive behavior makes them unsuitable for most private keepers and all novices.

Like most other African monitors, Nile monitors have strong jaw muscles that allow them to crush large snail shells.

Water Monitors

Water monitors are very similar to Nile monitors, except for two important differences. While water monitors are often relatively tame animals, they grow to enormous sizes – they are the second largest species in the world.

Even a "puppy-dog-tame" lizard measuring 6 or 7 feet in length is potentially dangerous. Additionally, they require very large cages – better described as small rooms.

Additionally, while they do not require a large water receptacle for survival, they spend much of their lives in the wild in water, so the keeper must consider whether or not they really want to keep an animal without providing a similar habitat to what they experience in the wild.

Water monitors can make suitable captives for very experienced keepers, with enough space to house these giants properly, but they are completely inappropriate for beginners.

Crocodile Monitors

Crocodile monitors are the longest – if not most massive – lizard species on the planet. They may exceed 8 feet in length, courtesy of their long tails, although they are lithe enough to live a primarily arboreal existence.

Crocodile monitors often have defensive personalities, and are equipped with a very large set of teeth. Many crocodile monitor keepers have sustained very serious injuries while tending their captives.

Only experienced keepers, zoo staff and similar individuals should attempt to keep crocodile monitors in captivity.

"New" Euprepiosaurus Species

Several new species have been described in the "mangrove monitor complex" over the last few years. While many of these new species are showing up in the pet trade, beginners should avoid these animals until more experienced keepers have devised husbandry protocols. Additionally, as these monitors are invariably wild caught, they are sure to have high parasite loads.

However, once they have been kept in captivity for some time, and many of these species may make suitable pets. Most remain modest in size, and appear to have relatively calm temperaments.

With luck, keepers will figure out how to breed many of these species, as their restricted geographic ranges make them susceptible to rapid population declines.

Chapter 18: Further Reading

Never stop learning more about your new pet's natural history, biology and captive care. Doing so will help you to provide your new pet with the highest quality of life possible.

Books

Bookstores and online book retailers often offer a treasure trove of information that will advance your quest for knowledge. While books represent an additional cost involved in reptile care, you can consider it an investment in your pet's well-being. Your local library may also carry some books about monitor lizards, which you can borrow for no charge.

University libraries are a great place for finding old, obscure or academically oriented books about monitor lizards. You may not be allowed to borrow these books if you are not a student, but you can view and read them at the library.

Herpetology: An Introductory Biology of Amphibians and Reptiles

By Laurie J. Vitt, Janalee P. Caldwell

Academic Press, 2013

Understanding Reptile Parasites: A Basic Manual for Herpetoculturists & Veterinarians

By Roger Klingenberg D.V.M.

Advanced Vivarium Systems, 1997

Infectious Diseases and Pathology of Reptiles: Color Atlas and Text

Elliott Jacobson

CRC Press

Designer Reptiles and Amphibians

Richard D. Bartlett, Patricia Bartlett

Barron's Educational Series

Monitor Lizards: Natural History, Biology and Husbandry

Daniel Bennett

Edition Chimaira

Varanoid Lizards of the World

Edited by Eric R. Pianka, Dennis King, Ruth Allen King

Indiana University Press

Dragons in the Dust: The Paleobiology of the Giant Monitor Lizard Megalania

Ralph E. Molnar

Indiana University Press

Monitors, Tegus and Related Lizards

Richard D. Bartlett

Barron's Educational Series

Monitor Lizards: Natural History, Captive Care and Breeding

Bernd Eidenmüller, Grant Husband

Edition Chimaira

Lizards: Windows to the Evolution of Diversity

By Eric R. Pianka, Laurie J. Vit

University of California Press

Goannas: The Biology of Varanid Lizards

By Dennis King, Brian Green

UNSW Press

Magazines

www.reptilesmagazine.com/

Covering reptiles commonly kept in captivity, kingsnakes are frequently featured in the magazine, and its online partner.

http://www.practicalreptilekeeping.co.uk/

Practical Reptile Keeping is a popular publication aimed at beginning and advanced hobbies. Topics include the care and maintenance of popular reptiles as well as information on wild reptiles.

Websites

With the explosion of the internet, it is easier to find information about reptiles than it has ever been. However, this growth has cause an increase in the proliferation of both good information and bad information.

While knowledgeable breeders, keepers and academics operate some websites, others lack the same dedication and scientific rigor. Anyone with a computer and internet connection can launch a website and say virtually anything they want about monitor lizards. Accordingly, as with all other research, consider the source of the information before making any husbandry decisions.

The Reptile Report

www.thereptilereport.com/

The Reptile Report is a news-aggregating website that accumulates interesting stories and features about reptiles from around the world.

Kingsnake.com

www.kingsnake.com

Started as a small website for gray-banded kingsnake enthusiasts, Kingsnake.com has become one of the largest reptile-oriented portals in the hobby. Includes classifieds, breeder directories, message forums and other resources.

The Vivarium and Aquarium News

www.vivariumnews.com/

The online version of the former publication, The Vivarium and Aquarium News provides in-depth coverage of different reptiles and amphibians in a captive and wild context.

Journals

Journals are the primary place professional scientists turn when they need to learn about monitor lizards. While they may not make light reading, hobbyists stand to learn a great deal from journals.

Herpetologica

www.hljournals.org/

Published by The Herpetologists' League, Herpetologica, and its companion publication, Herpetological Monographs cover all aspects of reptile and amphibian research.

Journal of Herpetology

www.ssarherps.org/

Produced by the Society for the Study of Reptiles and Amphibians, the Journal of Herpetology is a peer-reviewed publication covering a variety of reptile-related topics.

Copeia

www.asihcopeiaonline.org/

Copeia is published by the American Society of Ichthyologists and Herpetologists. A peer-reviewed journal, Copeia covers all aspects of the biology of reptiles, amphibians and fish.

Nature

www.nature.com/

Although Nature covers all aspects of the natural world, there is plenty for lizard enthusiasts.

Supplies
Big Apple Pet Supply

http://www.bigappleherp.com

Big Apple Pet Supply carries most common husbandry equipment, including heating devices, water dishes and substrates.

LLLReptile

http://www.lllreptile.com

LLL Reptile carries a wide variety of husbandry tools, heating devices, lighting products and more.

Doctors Foster and Smith

http://www.drsfostersmith.com

Foster and Smith is a veterinarian-owned retailer that supplies husbandry-related items to pet keepers.

Support Organizations

Sometimes, the best way to learn about monitor lizards is to reach out to other keepers and breeders. Check out these organizations, and search for others in your geographic area.

The National Reptile & Amphibian Advisory Council

http://www.nraac.org/

The National Reptile & Amphibian Advisory Council seeks to educate the hobbyists, legislators and the public about reptile and amphibian related issues.

American Veterinary Medical Association

www.avma.org

The AVMA is a good place for Americans to turn if you are having trouble finding a suitable reptile veterinarian.

The World Veterinary Association

http://www.worldvet.org/

The World Veterinary Association is a good resource for finding suitable reptile veterinarians worldwide.

References

Ast, J. C. (n.d.). *Varanidae*. Retrieved from Animal Diversity Web: http://animaldiversity.ummz.umich.edu/accounts/Varanidae/

Brian G. Fry, e. a. (2008). A central role for venom in predation by Varanus komodoensis (Komodo Dragon) and the extinct giant Varanus (Megalania) priscus. *PNAS*.

D, K. M. (1975). Chromosomal Evolution in the Lizard Genus Varanus (Reptilia). *Australian Journal of Biological Sciences*.

Greene, H. W. (1986). Diet and arboreality in the emerald monitor, Varanus prasinus, with comments on the study of adaptation. *Fieldiana Zoology*.

Phillips, S. M. (1997). Specific Dynamic Action of a Large Carnivorous Lizard, Varanus albigularis. *Comparative Biochemistry and Physiology Part A: Physiology*.

PIANKA, E. R. (2006). Comparative ecology of Varanus in the Great Victoria Desert. *Austral Ecology*.

Pianka, E. R. (n.d.). Notes on the Biology of Varanus eremius. *University of Western Australia*.

Smith, K. K. (2005). Morphology and function of the tongue and hyoid apparatus in Varanus (varanidae, lacertilia). *Journal of Morphology*.

Stephen C. Wood, K. J. (1974). Respiratory adaptations to diving in the nile monitor lizard,Varanus niloticus. *Journal of comparative physiology*.

TODD T. GLEESON, G. S. (n.d.). Cardiovascular responses to graded activity in the lizards Varanus and Iguana . *University of California*.

Williams, R. E. (1984). Ontogenetic variation in the molariform teeth of lizards. *Journal of Vertebrate Paleontology*.

Published by IMB Publishing 2015

Copyright and Trademarks. This publication is Copyright 2015 by IMB Publishing. All products, publications, software and services mentioned and recommended in this publication are protected by trademarks. In such instance, all trademarks & copyright belong to the respective owners. All rights reserved. No part of this book may be reproduced or transferred in any form or by any means, graphic, electronic, or mechanical, including photocopying, recording, taping, or by any information storage retrieval system, without the written permission of the author. Pictures used in this book are either royalty free pictures bought from stock-photo websites or have the source mentioned underneath the picture.

Disclaimer and Legal Notice. This product is not legal or medical advice and should not be interpreted in that manner. You need to do your own due-diligence to determine if the content of this product is right for you. The author and the affiliates of this product are not liable for any damages or losses associated with the content in this product. While every attempt has been made to verify the information shared in this publication, neither the author nor the affiliates assume any responsibility for errors, omissions or contrary interpretation of the subject matter herein. Any perceived slights to any specific person(s) or organization(s) are purely unintentional. We have no control over the nature, content and availability of the web sites listed in this book. The inclusion of any web site links does not necessarily imply a recommendation or endorse the views expressed within them. IMB Publishing takes no responsibility for, and will not be liable for, the websites being temporarily unavailable or being removed from the Internet. The accuracy and completeness of information provided herein and opinions stated herein are not guaranteed or warranted to produce any particular results, and the advice and strategies, contained herein may not be suitable for every individual. The author shall not be liable for any loss incurred as a consequence of the use and application, directly or indirectly, of any information presented in this work. This publication is designed to provide information in regard to the subject matter covered. The information included in this book has been compiled to give an overview of the subjects and detail some of the symptoms, treatments etc. that are available to canines with these conditions. It is not intended to give medical advice. For a firm diagnosis of your dog's condition, and for a treatment plan suitable for you, you should consult your veterinarian or consultant. The writer of this book and the publisher are not responsible for any damages or negative consequences following any of the treatments or methods highlighted in this book. Website links are for informational purposes only and should not be seen as a personal endorsement; the same applies to the products detailed in this book. The reader should also be aware that although the web links included were correct at the time of writing, they may become out of date in the future.